REFLECTIONS OF A RELUCTANT CLERIC

... another way of faith

CHARLES HOFFMAN

eFrog Press

To Sharon

CONTENTS

Preface

As I began to think about this exercise I felt it would be good to leave something in writing for my two sons and their families. I also wondered, usually secretly, if others might be interested in what I have to say. So I began the process of writing a book and presto—here it is.

Left to my own devices, I would never have chosen to become a cleric, a minister in the Christian church. I came to my calling with a great reluctance. Early on, such an idea was abhorrent to me. But decades later I concluded that I had been guided by a higher wisdom.

Over the course of my life various people encouraged me to write. One such person is William Fore, himself a writer, a leader in the church, and now retired. Bill came to worship with my congregation and on numerous occasions he would open our conversations with a question: what was I writing? He would not let me off the hook and his persistence motivated me to respond.

Another source of encouragement is my publisher, Linda Scott. Following my retirement I met Linda one day at a coffee shop. The meeting was not planned; we simply bumped into each other. She asked me what I was doing now that I was no longer a minister under appointment in the United Methodist Church. I told her, among other things, that I was writing. She asked to read a sample of my work, I complied, and she said that she would like to put what I was writing between the two covers of a book. Now it is done and I am grateful for the encouragement from Linda, Bill, and others.

I have not altered names of people and places in what follows. Nor have I protected the innocent. I would simply say that none of the names have been changed because we are all, in one way or another, guilty of life.

Finally, I want to say that Sharon, my wife and partner for fifty-six years, has also cheered me along. As an avid reader she supported my project and put up with the many mood swings that go into anything that comes close to creativity. Her opinions on my success, or lack of such, have always served me as a bottom line. On this point I am a man most fortunate, and I happily dedicate this effort to her.

Charles Hoffman,

October 7, 2016

1

A New Land and a New Life

On the third day of September in the year 1739, the sailing ship *Robert and Alice*, with canvases stressed and soiled and torn, finally appeared on the eastern horizon and was seen at last from the shores of America. Her captain was Walter Goodman, under whose firm hand she was about to complete the voyage from Europe, more precisely, from Rotterdam in Holland to Philadelphia in the New World. On board was a group of Germans from the Rhine River Valley in western Germany who, prior to their embarkation, had traveled down the river to the Dutch seaport. Their goal was a better and more secure life than any of them could imagine in their homeland. Religious, economic, and other issues, coupled with the promise of the British colonies in America, finally inspired them to seek their fortunes on the other side of the Atlantic.

I was on that ship, part of the German contingent,

and this is my attempt to tell my family's story, a tale whose roots reach back nearly three hundred years to this eighteenth-century voyage. The leader of our clan and a passenger on the *Robert and Alice* was John Peter Hoffman, my four-times-great-grandfather who was born in 1709. He was thirty years old at the time of his emigration.

Little can be ascertained with certainty about John Peter's life prior to this time, but we can be reasonably sure that he was a master carpenter, a man of robust health and of deep spirituality. In harmony with this period of the Enlightenment it is said that he championed the basic concept of the freedom of man, both politically and religiously. If this indeed was his posture on the subject, then he was out of step with the Reformed theology in which he was reared, but he was not alone in his philosophy of human self-determination. In his mind America, more than any other place he knew, promised fulfillment of his dreams for freedom of religion, politics, of conscience, and of a voice to express his personal points of view.

We do know that the ship he boarded for his Atlantic crossing was registered in Dublin, Ireland. But it was transporting Germans from the land of their birth to the British colonies in America, the land to which they had attached their aspirations and hopes and in which they would ultimately realize their destiny. For a variety of reasons my forefather, John Peter Hoffman, and his fellow travelers were leaving their homeland. They were following rivers that flowed into the Rhine and eventually emptied into the North Sea at Rotterdam. For these German émigrés, this was the gateway city to their rebirth in a new world.

In most, if not all, cases this was not a cruise to be enjoyed; it was an ordeal to be endured. Mercifully, it might last as little as eight weeks but it could be much longer, depending on sailing conditions and the time required for any number of bureaucratic demands that would have to be met before the oceanic crossing even began. Understandably, there were no extra charges for a longer passage. But there was an added intrinsic cost because whenever the crossing was prolonged, conditions on the ship worsened. The cramped quarters became harder to bear, the quality of the food deteriorated, and the water became scarce and often contaminated.

For some of the 180 passengers the trip would be fatal, their bodies and their dreams released together into the void of a vast ocean and lost forever in the depths of the sea. As is usually the case in dire situations such as these Germans faced, those most vulnerable to such an outcome were the very young and the very old. Others, when the ship finally docked in Philadelphia, were too weak to disembark without assistance. And then there were the first months in the colonies: the adjustments, the exposure to disease, and more dying. Many of the immigrants could not afford the price of the passage, so they borrowed funds and signed agreements to pay their debts by indentured servitude and too often were thereby subjected to the exploitations of unprincipled masters. But in spite of the risks and realities, the Germans came. From the second half of the seventeenth century and through most of the eighteenth century, German migration to the new land surged. In fact, during the 1700s more Germans than English moved to

America. And by 1917, the year the United States entered what was called the Great War, there were more people of German ancestry than British or Irish in America.

Today, in the early years of the twenty-first century, citizens of German origin number more than fifty million. Most of those who came at the beginning of the resettlement made their homes in Pennsylvania. So, by the year 1775, they accounted for one-third of the Pennsylvania colony's population, nearly sixty thousand making their new home in the growing city of Philadelphia. The majority of these came from the southwest part of Germany as we see it today on the map. This area is often referred to as the Palatinate, a title derived from the fact that the region had, at one time or another, been under the jurisdiction of one or more secular princes of the Holy Roman Empire known as counts palatine. These Germans landed in the New World in three great waves of migration, crashing onto the shore of their chosen destination exhausted, spent, demoralized, and short of funds. If they were fortunate, there would be friends or relatives to help finance their travel and guide their initial faltering steps toward a better future. If not, only their own heroic efforts could get them there. Surely, they knew in advance that it would be hard. So the hopeful decision to come was laden with liability; it was not a casual journey to be undertaken lightly. There was simply too much at stake.

When historians chronicle reasons why people leave their native country and move to another, they refer to what are called the *push* and the *pull* factors—things that repel potential emigrants away from where they are and things that attract them to where they might be. These factors were definitely at work among many Europeans during the 1700s, the century of mass migrations.

At that time Germany was not a united country as it is today. Within its borders were smaller kingdoms, principalities, duchies, estates, and other feudalistic arrangements, each with its own measure of autonomy and authority. And in too many instances the common people suffered the arbitrary whims of those who owned the land and wielded the power. These landowners tended to make things difficult for their subjects and essentially crushed any hopes they harbored for a better life. In the long passage of time this has often been so—as the rich flourish, the poor fail. So the simple truth is that hardships of the homeland pushed people to seek another way, another venue in which to realize their lives and raise their families.

Contrast their plight with the temptation of vast and available spaces in America, along with the loose reins of absentee rulers, the light taxations, and the guaranteed freedoms, including the freedom to worship God according to one's conscience, and it is easy to understand why people were pulled west from Europe, from the British Isles, and from Ireland to America. Clearly, for these immigrants there were many reasons to leave home: political constraints, economic hardships, religious intolerance, a shortage of farmland, and the inability of their particular part of the world to support the growing population. For these realities at least, many made the hard choice to turn their backs on their homes, their friends, and oftentimes their families and to set their sights on a promising future on the other side of the immense ocean to the west.

But they did not all venture to the west; in the case of the Germans, most of them went east. Between 1680 and 1790, about 400,000 immigrated to places like Hungary and Prussia and Russia. A much smaller number, about 100,000, came to America. These immigrants were influenced by letters from those who were already there. Many times the letters were read aloud in public houses, correspondence that extolled the advantages of a place where good land was both available and affordable. And there was another factor at work that pulled these Germans toward America. It had become clear to enterprising sea merchants that transporting these people and their families to the New World was a lucrative business. So companies that owned and operated the ships advertised and even overstated the potential advantages of the burgeoning transatlantic world. They stood to realize a considerable profit by exploiting the situation, even if it meant the inevitable trysts with fierce Atlantic storms.

To people with little or no chance of obtaining sustainable employment and with no prospects of owning sufficient land for farming, the appeal of America had to be considered. And it was. For many, America was simply too seductive to be resisted. The lure of a farmer having his own land to cultivate or of a craftsman having his own business to pursue was overwhelming temptation. And so, from the waterways of the Rhine River and its tributaries, Germans left their villages, somehow made their way to the seaport city of Rotterdam, and set their faces toward a new land and a new life. It must have been a fearfully exciting experience to contemplate the journey, decide to take the risk, board the vessel, endure the rigors of sailing, and finally complete the crossing.

By the year 1776, according to historian David McCullough, America had a higher standard of living than any people in the world. The Germans who came here at this time could not have known this, but they sensed that something highly desirable was taking place across the water and they wanted a part in it. Among those willing to risk everything and set their hearts on America were my ancestor John Peter Hoffman, who was familiarly known as Peter; and three of his brothers: Martin, Johannes, and Daniel. Their names appear on the ship manifest of the *Robert and Alice,* which docked in Philadelphia in the late summer of 1739.

I have reason to believe that John Peter and his brothers entered the Rhine River near the present city of Mainz, Germany, to begin the downstream journey to Rotterdam. They probably paid the fare to be transported to their Dutch destination by some enterprising riverboat captain. Perhaps they made their way on a freighter and paid for the ride by working on the ship as it loaded and unloaded cargo along the way.

In whatever way they navigated the Rhine, it must have been an awesome experience. Having grown up in the hinterland west of Mainz, it is conceivable that none of them had ever been to the city. Mainz was in those days and is today located on the west bank of the northerly flowing river. By the middle of the eighteenth century, when John Peter and the others were riding the river current toward their rendezvous with the oceanic crossing, Mainz was known for its large and influential Jewish population. However, the city had a history of anti-Semitism. Jews in Mainz had been banished from the city on more than one occasion, a despicable practice carried out in other parts of Europe as well as in Germany. In Mainz they had been used as scapegoats and blamed for the outbreak of what was then called the Black Death. Meanwhile, the Christians had built their extravagant churches, including the Romanesque Mainz Cathedral, already seven hundred years old when the Hoffman party sailed past her. I wonder how much of this the brothers were aware of. Did they take notice of the cathedral, an edifice built over hundreds of years, probably with an inordinate measure of the cost shouldered by the poor? Were they aware of the sordid history of misdeeds toward the Jews, or were they so intent on getting down the river that they missed the stories of history that confronted them at every bend of the river? In the little that I have learned about John Peter, it is easy for me to think that he *was* aware of his world, that he took notice of its injustices, that he respected the simple truth that each person carries within himself or herself something of the divine image, and that he was not willing to accept the deplorable conditions in which so many persons fought for basic survival.

Now, after sailing past Mainz they came to Koblenz, a city of historic French invasions located at the place where the Mosel River flows into the Rhine. Then came Bonn, the city where Ludwig van Beethoven would be born some thirty years later, and where they might have seen the towering steeple of the Bonn Minster, a church dating back to the eleventh century. In front of this church were statues of the severed heads of two martyred saints, Cassius and Florentius. These two had been followers of another martyr who bears the oxymoronic title of *military saint.* This one is known as Saint Gereon, and his statue, another severed head, lies outside the Minor Basilica in Cologne that bears his name. Saint Gereon is appealed to by those suffering from migraine headaches. There must be a lesson here but I am not sure I know what it is.

Cologne was next on the list of cities my ancestor viewed as he navigated the Rhine River. Here, he and his brothers saw the great yet unfinished Gothic cathedral on their starboard side—a monument dedicated to housing the bones of the Three Wise Men whose visit to the infant Jesus has been immortalized in scripture and tradition. Construction on the church had begun in 1248 and was brought to a halt in 1473, not to be completed until the nineteenth century. When the Hoffman siblings saw the great structure only half of the construction was completed. It had been a massive undertaking, much more than its original builders could imagine, and they had failed to complete the job. I wonder if the lesson had been lost on these intrepid seamen. Or did they say, "Unlike those hopeful cathedral builders, we will see our project through to a successful conclusion; we will not surrender our dreams. We will arrive in our new world and there we will make a new life for ourselves and for the families we envision. May God help us."

There were more cityscapes along the way but in the course of that summer Rotterdam at last came into view.

The foundation had been laid and the superstructure could begin. So, it was now time to book passage for America, a challenge that could take a significant amount of time and, depending on how much time, could force them into the unfavorable weather of fall and winter for the Atlantic voyage. Added to this was the fact that, prior to proceeding to the colonies in America, their ship would take them to Britain, where they would secure their official immigration papers. Meanwhile, the Atlantic storms were poised and waiting to pounce. As things turned out, these Germans successfully navigated all the bureaucratic hurdles, wrapped up the red tape, and embarked on the definitive part of their adventure, crossing the great Atlantic.

What might be forgotten about this enterprise is that the immigrants were not the only ones to profit from their movement to America. The advantages of this German migration applied not only to the newcomers themselves; the benefits flowed in two directions. So, while the colonies offered these immigrants realistic hope for improvement, their coming to America greatly enriched their land of choice. And as a class of people, the Germans were better educated and more literate than any other group of immigrants. Most of them were farmers whose good reputation preceded them. Many of them were accomplished craftsmen and artisans. There is a consensus among historians that these German newcomers brought with them a vast wealth of skills in farming and in craftsmanship that proved invaluable to the new country.

And so it is that in the mix of political, social, religious, economic, and other realities I find my own European roots. I look back on a thirty-year-old German adventurer boarding a ship at a busy Dutch port. His destination is the burgeoning port in the city of brotherly love, the land of William Penn. He trusts that the voyage will lead not only to a new land, but to a new life of opportunity and hope. But there are no guarantees. Who knows what he was thinking as he watched the ship's gangplank being lifted and the lines to the dock loosened and the connections to his homeland severed forever? Who knows how he felt when, after weeks of sailing, he finally placed his feet on the soil of America, buoyed by its potential yet burdened by its challenge? Who knows what hardships and what fears he must have faced during the first steps of a journey undertaken with no clear map to guide its course?

Walter Goodman was in charge and the young German passenger was John Peter Hoffman, my great-great-great-great-grandfather. His bravery—some would say his audacity—in undertaking such a journey planted my family in the Pennsylvania colony. He was a pioneer and progenitor of those people who came to be known as the Pennsylvania Dutch or, more accurately, the Pennsylvania Germans.

Today there is a large tombstone standing in a farm field in Dauphin County, Pennsylvania, nestled in a place called Lykens Valley. There is no footpath to the monument. If you want to get there you simply walk through the grain field. The inscription etched into the six-foot-tall granite stone tells the story and reads as follows:

John Peter Hoffman
—Pioneer—
—Arrived From Holland In 1739—
—Settled Here 1759—
Born 1709—Died 1798
His Remains With Those Of 26 Contemporaries
Lie Buried Here
Erected By The Hoffman Association—1924

I stood by that memorial stone one gray and bitterly cold January day at the beginning of the new millennium, the twenty-first century. The winter wind dusted skiffs of snow across the forlorn countryside. As events converged, the scene was an ominous reflection of the landscape of my life at that moment in time. Less than a month earlier, I had lost my older brother to a felon's gun in the high desert of Sonora, Mexico. A dark grief hovered over my soul. I recalled the words of William Shakespeare:

"Blow, blow, thou winter wind.
Thou art not so unkind
As man's ingratitude."

And I remember that in that poignant moment something stirred within me. It was a sense of gratitude, a feeling of hope and thankfulness. It happened in spite of my bleak and broken spirit. I will always remember laying my cold hand on that cold stone and whispering my thanks, my gratitude to this man named John Peter Hoffman, my greatest grandfather, for bringing me to America, for giving me life and opening up the endless possibilities life has to offer.

It was a good bad day, which is a way of describing all of life, his and mine. It is a mingling of joy and sorrow, of good and bad, pleasure and pain, of gain and loss. And it is of this I want to tell in what follows.

2

SETTLED IN AMERICA

Details about the life of John Peter Hoffman are understandably sketchy given the fact that he was born more than three centuries ago. However, one thing I know for sure is that counting from his generation to mine, we represent seven generations of the family in America. On April 9, 1743, less than four years after his arrival in Philadelphia, my four-times-great-grandfather married a Pennsylvania German woman named Maria Sarah Schneider. To John Peter and Maria Sarah were born eight children, including my ancestor, Christian.

As a matter of much interest for me personally, I have seen one genealogy that makes John Peter a direct descendent of a Johann Hoffman (1371–1479), who, along with Johann Otto von Munsterberg, played a major role in establishing Leipzig University. It would please me to learn that my roots truly do reach back to such an august figure as this founder of what is today the second-oldest university in Germany, dating to the year 1409, and claiming a long list of distinguished alumni including the poet Goethe, the composer Wagner, the philosopher Nietzsche, nine Nobel Prize winners, and German chancellor Angela Merkel.

Not so well known among the prominent names of famous Leipzig students is a man by the name of Luz Long. Aptly named, Luz Long was a world-class athlete, a long jumper who competed in the Berlin Olympics of 1936—Adolf Hitler's grand spectacle by which he planned to showcase the superiority of the Aryan race. Unfortunately for the Nazi leader, his prize Olympian was in competition with an African American athlete named Jesse Owens. As the story unfolded, it was the German Luz Long who, upon seeing Owens on the verge of failing to qualify for the final competition in the long jump and in an act of uncommon sportsmanship, actually coached his archrival in a successful attempt to qualify. Long's advice to Owens worked. Then, having both qualified, the two great jumpers met in head-to-head competition in the final for Olympic long jump champion. Owens defeated Long to earn one of his four gold medals; Long placed second and took the Olympic silver. Sadly, within a few years Luz Long was killed in Hitler's great gamble to bring all of Europe and Russia under his control.

I would be thrilled to know as a certainty that my fifteenth-century ancestor played such a key role in the founding of the prestigious university, but unless there is further corroboration I must leave the matter in the realm of wishful thinking.

John Peter Hoffman was born in what is known today as the German state of Rhineland-Palatinate, its capital being the city of Mainz. His birth took place in the village of Riegenroth, and he was christened February 17, 1709, in the church at Pleizenhausen. Both Riegenroth and Pleizenhausen are located to the northwest of Mainz, a short distance west of the Rhine River. The modern state of Rhineland-Palatinate is bordered on its western flank by France, Luxemburg, and Belgium.

There is some record of the life of John Peter's family in America. Fortunately, significant details have been preserved through the Hoffman Family Association—an informal group of John Peter's descendants who hold annual family reunions at the Hoffman's St. Peter's Church near the stone memorial in Lykens Valley. Actually, the Hoffman story is not unusual; it parallels the ancestral records of many American families who came here from the European continent and the British Isles during the 1700s, common people who were faced with formidable challenges. I can imagine very few of them went out of their way to do heroic things. This is simply the way things unfolded as they labored to fashion a life in their new home. They were forced to respond to unusual events—unexpected developments that relentlessly surprised and challenged them. It was a question of survival.

John Peter was thirty years old when he arrived at his chosen destination in the American colonies, historically an age when many life-altering decisions have been made. Personally, birthday number thirty was an event that I will never forget. It was unlike any other birthday for me. It was daunting, demoralizing, and somewhat frightening. I turned thirty in 1969, during the decade of student demonstrations and iconoclastic youth upheavals, and at a time when a common slogan of the populist movement advised the young not to trust anyone over thirty. Up to that point I was blithely going through the motions, following my own loosely scripted timetable; I acted as though life was endless and that I was immune to its hardships. So age thirty brought a devastating dose of reality as I came to terms with the simple fact that time limits our options and increases the risk of unmanageable developments visiting us. The moment had arrived for me to get on with what I wanted to accomplish; if I lived this long again I would arrive at the inconceivable age of sixty. For me, age thirty was Robert Frost's memorable divergence of two roads in the woods, a fork in the road. Standing there, at my thirtieth birthday, I knew it was time to choose my road, my path.

I believe it's a common experience at this juncture of life to be confronted by a wake-up call. It is true for commoners and for famous people as well. Martin Luther, the German priest who publicly protested against the excesses as well as the oversights of his Roman Catholic Church, embarked on his controversial historic enterprise not long after his thirtieth birthday. Centuries before Luther's time, a leader known as Augustine of Hippo did a similar thing. Although raised as a Christian, he had embarked on a life of hedonism as a young man. Born in 354 CE, he eventually presented himself for baptism into the church at the age of thirty-three. In subsequent years he distinguished himself as a pious scholar, leader, and teacher and is known in our times as Saint Augustine. A much more recent example of one who responded to a great mission at age thirty is Martin Luther King Jr. (1929–1968). At age thirty-three he was already working alongside the president of the United States in pushing the agenda for civil rights. A year later he delivered his famous "I Have a Dream" speech, and at age thirty-five he received the Nobel Peace Prize. There are others who fit the profile, including Moses the lawgiver and David the king in the Hebrew Bible. Add to this Jesus of Nazareth, whom scholars say was baptized at about the age of thirty and who then began his brief ministry along the shores of Galilee and the banks of the Jordan River in what is known today as Israel by some and Palestine by others.

John Peter Hoffman fits into this profile of people who made life-altering decisions near the onset of their fourth decade of life. My ancestor was a contemporary of the founder of my branch of the Christian church, an Englishman named John Wesley (1703–1791), for whom the age of thirty was also a turning point. Wesley, along with his younger brother Charles (1707–1788), was an Oxford University-educated Anglican priest who inspired efforts to found the movement known as Methodism within the Anglican establishment. Their contemporary, John Peter Hoffman, was born at a time when German immigration to America entered one of its most active periods, a first wave of mass migration that was continued during much of his century. It is not too much to say that John Peter's work and that of the Wesley brothers would directly and indirectly contribute to the early founding, growth, and development of America as a nation.

Wesley's movement was perfectly adapted to the frontier as his followers kept pace with the westward advance of the new country. So it is easy to document the vital role these Methodists played in addressing social issues such as slavery, labor injustice, health, and poverty. A large part of Wesley's genius was his methodical training of lay preachers whose mission was to keep pace with the settlers as they probed deeper and deeper into the uncharted corners of the new continent. These lay preachers were known as circuit riders, and their exploits are legendary as they crisscrossed the frontier on their horses. For example, the story is told of a settler who, with his family, had moved to the western frontier and almost immediately found himself confronted by one of John Wesley's mounted emissaries. The settler lamented his bad luck, said that he had moved west to get away from such preachers, and now, before he had even unloaded his wagon, here was another of these pesky Methodists. The rider was quick with a response. "You can't get rid of us," he said. "If you go to heaven you'll find us there; if you go to hell, I'm afraid you'll find us there as well. And seeing how it appears we are everywhere on Earth, you'd better come to terms with us."

It could well be an apocryphal story, but the tale reflects the spirit of these early American circuit riders, their infectious passion, their dedication, and their eagerness to set the new country on a sound course. This chronicle of the inveterate pioneer and the unwelcome preacher is an accurate portrayal of those early American followers of John Wesley.

To this day a great many American institutions owe their existence to public-minded Methodists, followers of these earlier circuit riders, who paid the price to bring them to life. Colleges and hospitals, initially established by John Wesley's followers, can be found all over the North American continent. A small sampling of these includes Syracuse University in New York State; Southern Methodist University in Dallas; the University of Southern California in Los Angeles; the University of Denver; Methodist University Hospital in Memphis; Duke University; Boston University; Claremont School of Theology; University of the Pacific in Stockton, California; Bethune-Cookman University in Daytona Beach, Florida; Iliff School of Theology in Denver; Rust College in Holly Springs, Mississippi; and many, many more. The complete list is truly overwhelming.

But long before this Methodist contribution there were the German immigrants. Their farms were emulated, their skills as craftsmen were needed, and their combined efforts played a determinative role in the colonists' break with England. Among this number was my forefather, who landed here in 1739, two hundred years prior to my own birth in 1939. He and I are separated by six generations.

I know that John Peter, both by experience and temperament, was well suited for his daring venture. He was a skilled carpenter and craftsman, as was my grandfather in his time and as is my older son today. Not only that, John Peter used his expertise to assist other immigrants in building homes on their chosen frontier, and he labored alongside others to clear land on which neat German farms could take shape, sustaining life through animal husbandry and the harvesting of fruit and vegetables, corn, and wheat. I know about those German farms firsthand from my childhood in the Fraser River Valley of British Columbia. German Mennonite farms were everywhere and the German tradition of utilitarian beauty was much in evidence. As a child I reluctantly picked strawberries and raspberries on those farms. My remuneration was five cents for each pound picked. I remember one of the growers I worked for as a man of great kindness and patience. At the end of the week he would drive a group of us young laborers to our homes an hour away, and I'm afraid we took his kind gesture for granted. On one ride home he told us about his love for Handel's *Messiah* and about how much he enjoyed sitting alone in a room listening to recordings of the oratorio. At the time I was in my early teens and I had never so much as heard of Handel or his music. Such was the impoverished cultural climate in which I spent my early years. But fortunately for me, it was not too many years until I had the opportunity to learn Handel's music and to participate in choirs that performed the composition.

Incidentally, the very first performance of *Messiah* took place at Saint Patrick's Cathedral in Dublin, Ireland, in the year 1742. Interestingly, the family of Arthur Guinness, founder of the Guinness breweries, were supporters of the cathedral, and there is also record of John Wesley having preached there.

Returning to John Peter Hoffman, we find him eleven years into the American undertaking. The year was 1750 and he was beginning the task of settling his family in the Lykens Valley, the site where the stone memorial to his life is located today. Since his arrival in America in 1739, he had made his American home in Berks County near Philadelphia where he plied his trade as a carpenter. Lykens Valley lies thirty miles northeast of what is now Harrisburg, Pennsylvania, and the valley continues to this day as an agricultural region. It received its English name after two of John Peter's contemporaries, John and Andrew *Lycans*; *Lykens* being a corruption of the original name. As with many American sites, however, the valley once bore an authentically American name: to the Native Americans it was known as Wiconisco, and you can still find that name used in the region. Surrounding the area are rolling hills and off to the east, standing guard over the pleasant landscape, is Short Mountain, aptly named as its elevation is no more than two thousand feet above sea level. Refreshing the valley's plants, trees, and animals in those early days was the Wiconisco Creek.

This gracious land must have seemed like a Garden of Eden to Hoffman and the other settlers. Here was virgin wilderness pulsating with life. The creeks and ponds were home to mallard ducks, swans, cormorants, herons, and Canada geese, along with beavers and muskrats. Bald eagles, hawks, and owls feasted on fish and small mammals such as squirrels, chipmunks, and cottontail rabbits. The forests of aspen and birch, oak and elm, walnut and willow, magnolia and maple, cedar and spruce and sycamore painted the land with endless shades of green before yielding to the alluring display of autumn colors. Pheasants and wild turkeys roamed the forest floor along with white-tailed deer, red foxes, and black bears. Flowers of unimaginable variety lifted their full palate of colors while the air above coursed its way through the wings of a hundred species of birds.

As John Peter's eyes first fell on this abundant scene at the foot of the mountain he must have been encouraged, and maybe even somewhat overwhelmed. Perhaps he experienced a moment when he knew, beyond doubt, that this was why he had staked everything—his family, his fortune, his future, his very life—risked it all and won. The hazards paid off. The scene unfolding before him as he looked deeper and deeper into its contours and hues was all the confirmation he needed. Here, indeed, was a world worth cultivating, especially to German immigrants for whom the scarcity of land had been a compelling reason to leave the fatherland. Traveling three thousand miles to seek a better place undoubtedly seemed foolhardy to many who stayed behind. But this scene, now stretching through the valley against the backdrop of Short Mountain, suggested that their stubborn resolution was sound. In a way that they had never before experienced, they were home.

3

UNSETTLED IN AMERICA

The early years in Lykens Valley were peaceful and productive as the newcomers began to establish themselves. On various occasions, Hoffman was paid visits by Native Americans of the Delaware Nation, which, at the time, were under the subjugation of the Iroquois Nation. Apparently, the Delaware visits were cordial and a mutual respect developed between these original Americans and some, but not all, of the newcomers from Europe. And, although there were a number of settlers in the valley besides the family of John Peter Hoffman, there seemed to be a special bond between him and the Delaware leaders. Other Lykens Valley residents with European, if not German, connections included John and Andrew Lycans, Ludwig Shott, and John Rewalt.

At that particular moment in the period of transition life was good—filled with promise, cradled in fertile land,

and shared with cordial native people and European neighbors. I can imagine there was among these early people a feeling of finally grasping the first fruits of their long journey to a new home. Finally, they were settled.

But it didn't last very long. In 1756, Hoffman and his neighbors in the Lykens Valley were driven off the land by the Iroquois. Once again, it's an old story—fighting over the question of land ownership. Mark Twain once said, "There is not an acre of ground on the globe that is in the possession of its rightful owner." It's hard to prove him wrong.

An event from these early days of the Lykens settlement focuses the situation that confronted the settlers. It was an early March morning that first year in the valley. As one of the Lycans brothers and John Rewalt ventured out to look after their cattle they were fired on by a small group of Iroquois. And as the firing continued the settlers ran for the Lycanses' cabin. Fortunately, the shots went wild and the men escaped unhurt. But a battle ensued in which others of the settlers joined in the skirmish, at least three of the Iroquois were killed, and three of the settlers were wounded. John Peter Hoffman, who had heard the gunfire from a distance, somehow made his way to the cabin, helped assess the situation, and agreed with the others that they should flee the scene before the Native Americans came back with reinforcements. So they made their way to Hanover Township, where they found safety with friends and where the three injured pioneers were treated for their wounds and subsequently recovered.

With this development in their American dream, the German settlers once more questioned the wisdom of their choice to come to America. Their emotions moved from the elation of their chosen Lykens Valley to the desperation of their flight from the hostile natives. But there was no turning back. No matter how bleak the prospect, they had to press on.

So, two years later, Hoffman and his family felt it was safe to return to the valley. Once there, Hoffman saw that many of the cabins and outbuildings had been burned by the Iroquois. But when he arrived at his own farm he found everything intact. Two rails had been set at the door to form an "X" and three notches had been cut in each end of the rails. As it turned out, this had been done by Delaware Indians as a reminder to the Iroquois that there lived a friend whose buildings were not to be disturbed.

During this period of conflict with some of the Native Americans, John Peter had become a soldier in what was called the Provincial Forces. The task of the forces was to oppose the native challenge and reclaim the lost land for the settlers. Knowing that the Native Americans might move against them at any moment meant that it was a disconcerting time for the new Americans. However, with the success of the Provincial Forces and over the course of the next four decades, Hoffman and his family rooted and shaped their lives in the Lykens Valley where they still have a presence to this day.

What John Peter and thousands of other immigrants to the colonies could not have known when they established their plans to start anew in America is that they would play an important role in one of history's most determinative wars, the American War of Independence from the British.

How many of them would have gone elsewhere or at least have stayed home had they known what awaited them? The burdens of survival in this new land were many; they came in a variety of forms and they were often intimidating. The last thing these people needed was another challenge added to what they already had.

But that is precisely what they got.

Here is a narrative deeply embedded in the American dream—the insistent pursuit of freedom and peace. My ancestors had crossed a vast ocean at great expense. They were chasing a compelling vision for a better life, one less burdensome and more promising. And the cruel irony is that they were soon thrown into the hellish violence of war. Freedom, if it were to come at all, would come at an awful price. And in order to pay that price, peace and tranquility and the basic human desire to achieve the fundamental things of life, something later and famously referred to as "the pursuit of happiness," would be profoundly threatened. In this my ancestors shared the experience of many of the world's immigrants and refugees. In this case the landscape of their promised land was littered with the troublesome fallout from the conflict between the British rulers and those who rebelled against injustices they could no longer endure. Thomas Paine put it succinctly when he wrote about the absurdity of a continent being ruled by an island, a sentiment shared by most of the colonists.

For some of the newcomers the situation was exacerbated by a piece of British legislation affecting all immigration to the colonies from the year 1727 and onward through the remaining years when America existed as a British colony.

The new law required the swearing of an oath of allegiance to the British Crown. Without this, clearance for travel to America would not be granted to those who pinned their hopes on what the colonies had to offer. Obviously, this created a moral dilemma for those who found themselves caught up in discussions about and ultimately actions geared toward breaking bonds with that same Crown.

Still another factor that impacted the German immigrant response to the ever-louder calls for American independence had to do with the British royal family's affiliations with Germans of the Hanover family. This British/German alliance influenced some of the Germans to side with Britain's King George III. They were not alone in their choice; many British and Dutch also struggled over the question of loyalty to the Crown. It was an awkward moment in history, preferences were divided, and it was not always easy to know which way to tilt with one's decision.

In spite of all the complexities, most of the German immigrants took up the patriot cause. Two of John Peter Hoffman's sons served as soldiers in the American Revolution. John (1746–1831), his eldest son, was commander of what was called the Upper Paxtang Company on a 1778 Susquehanna River expedition. Earlier, in 1763, he had played a part in the Battle of Muncy Hills, a land conflict between settlers and Native Americans. John Peter's third son, Christian (1752–1839), through whom I trace my own ancestry, also served in the Revolutionary army.

Many American citizens of German, Dutch, Scotch, and Irish ancestry recount similar histories about ancestors enrolled in George Washington's revolutionary forces. There is nothing particularly unusual about this. But there were others who, while they never took up arms in the struggle, contributed heroically to the cause of freedom. Often, what is not known is the extent to which these noncombatant patriots, in particular the Germans, contributed to the war effort through the variety and extent of the materiel they supplied to the ragtag army of General George Washington.

Historians call attention to the German contributions: rifles, bayonets, canons cast by Pennsylvania Germans, shot and shells, gunpowder, wagons for the transfer of goods, horses, clothing and uniforms, milled flour, medical support; all this and more was abundantly supplied by the new German Americans. Of course, it was not enough. The patriots suffered from shortages in just about every way. But it would have been much worse had it not been for the industry of the Germans and others in their support of the effort for independence.

These American patriots from Germany stand out in sharp contrast to the Hessians, thirty thousand German mercenaries who were recruited by King George III in his attempt to stop the American push for self-rule. Obviously, these hired guns were not able to tip the scales in the king's favor and ended up as part of the losing side. Thousands of Hessians died in the war and were buried in unmarked graves near the battlegrounds where they fell. Noteworthy is the fact that some six thousand of the surviving Hessians opted to remain in America when the war ended; they had seen enough to make them desire a share in the new republic.

Clearly, at this time in history, the Hoffman family was firmly and permanently settling into its adopted home; there would be no turning back. John Peter himself lived to see the day when General George Washington became the first president of the newly formed United States of America.

In the years to follow, generation after generation entered into the larger story of America with its patchwork of diverse people. My own American history, starting with the German immigrant, continues through his son, Christian Hoffman, his sixth child and third son. Christian married a woman named Susanna Diebler, born the same year as her husband. She and Christian had thirteen children and my ancestry relates to their twelfth child, Philip Grant Luther Hoffman (1811–1881). The interesting thing about Philip is that he was a contemporary of President Abraham Lincoln and served as a private in the Grand Army of the Republic in the Civil War. He married Catherine Ziegler (1814–1861), and to them was born my great-grandfather, Peter Albright Hoffman (1850–1927), their ninth child. Peter Albright married my great-grandmother, Mary Smith. Their son, my grandfather, was William Cyrus Hoffman (1878–1971), who married my grandmother, Emily Blanche Snook (1888–1976), on December 8, 1906. These two, my Hoffman grandparents, had eleven children, nine of whom survived to marry and raise families of their own. My father, Willard Franklin Hoffman, was second oldest of the nine surviving children of William and Blanche.

All my life I heard the stories. This one is about the twins, the first two children born to my paternal grandparents, William and Blanche. Their names were Robert Albright

Hoffman and Mary Elizabeth Hoffman and they lived only a few hours; they survived less than a day. What I heard was that Grandfather buried the babies in an unmarked grave on the plains near Gladys, North Dakota. As far as I can determine, there is no official record of their deaths, my uncle Robert and aunt Mary whose brief lives ended bitterly on the day they were born.

As I write this I am struck once again by the harsh reality of existence for my ancestors. It humbles me to think of all they endured so that my family and I could enjoy so much, and I am deeply grateful for the spirit of these hardy pioneers. I think especially of the women who were born and bred to surrender to the will of their men at every turn. How these strong women must have suffered and how they must have struggled to hold their tongues and leave their ideas unvoiced, whether good or bad. Theirs was to submit, to go along with their partner, many times to suffer silently through the deprivations and, too often, the bad decisions they were not allowed to question. Of course, many of them did not survive; they died young after twenty or thirty years of unremitting toil, endless pregnancies, and broken spirits.

Witness the lives of my grandparents, William and Blanche Hoffman. I have often said that my grandfather was a man who was always happy where he was not. He was born not far from the Lykens Valley at a place called Carsonville, Pennsylvania, which is located on the famous Appalachian Trail. That trail seduces hundreds of trekkers each year to test their mettle on its three thousand miles of footpaths. Who knows? Perhaps my grandfather's proximity to the trail accounts for his itchy feet, his wanderlust that was always ahead of him. He could not decide where to settle down.

When Grandfather was a single young man he moved from Pennsylvania to North Dakota where he eventually married my grandmother. Although she was also from the Keystone State, they met for the first time out west in North Dakota. Her family had moved there in 1903 when she was fifteen. Three years later William and Blanche married and settled in a village called Gladys. It was here that my grandparents' first surviving child, Harvey Clair, was born in 1908. Some time after this they returned briefly to Pennsylvania.

In 1910, having learned of the availability of land to homestead in Canada, they left the east and once again journeyed west where Grandfather filed for land in Saskatchewan, a short distance north of the international border from Grandmother's family, who now lived in Williston, North Dakota.

My father, Willard Franklin, was born in the autumn of that year. Two years later his sister Jennie Mae was born and two years after that, a brother named Norman Edward. The three births took place in the family home, a house Grandfather built out of prairie sod on a quarter section of land, 160 acres that comprised the homestead.

Willard and his siblings represent the sixth generation of our German family in America. After six generations I would have thought that he, Aunt Jennie, and Uncle Norman deserved something better than a sod house rising out of the bleak prairie from which to make their entrance into the twentieth century. People today think of babies being born in sterile hospitals with state-of-the-art equipment and expert medical care. And in North America this is usually the way of things.

Sadly, this is not true for most of the world's mothers and their babies. Births occur in mud huts and straw shacks and even in the fields where the women toil anonymously. Some children come into the world as their mothers flee toward the relative safety of a crude refugee camp. Some are born to frightened mothers who are children themselves and cannot understand what has happened to them. For far too many, the chances of survival are slim at best. So my father, his sister, and his brother are in good company in the sod house. In fact, it was said of another baby, born long before Father and his siblings, that his birth took place in a manger because there was no room in the inn.

Most of what I have related here is duplicated in the growth rings of every family tree. Most people who hear such family stories quickly move on to today and tomorrow and leave the past to bury the past. But I am not one of those people; I believe it matters that we know from whence we have come. Some of us desire and are able to memorialize this part of who we are—in biblical times "to raise an Ebenezer"—a sort of monument to that part of our lives that passed this way before. We do not forget the good times, the moments of elation and of unfettered joy. But we also remember the obstacles, the gut-wrenching losses, the horizons devoid of hope with which our families have persevered and somehow prevailed. I want to believe that I am one of those who remember the good and the bad.

So, I mark a special place called family, a kinship bound by special memories of my forbearers. With this writing I remove my shoes because I know that the soil on which I stand is holy, bought and blessed by those who got here first and pioneered a place that is uniquely mine.

What is it that ushered me to this life—random chance, good fortune, loving providence—who knows? My very existence hangs by a slender cord. My German-born ancestor might have perished before he ever saw the shore of the American colony. His third child, Christian, who was my three-times-great-grandfather, might have lost his life in the war of the American Revolution. Christian's twelfth child of thirteen, Philip Grant Luther, was my great-great-grandfather who was a member of the Grand Army of the Republic during America's Civil War. There are so many things that had to take place before I could even be born. What if my grandmother had died in childbirth, an all too common tragedy in that time? What if my father had perished as a child suffering through the brutal prairie winters with not enough food and inadequate clothing? These and a thousand other happenstances could have gone wrong and made my life impossible, this life that I have loved and treasured for more than seventy years.

So I take none of it for granted, not those things that occurred nor those that did not. In some mysterious way the planets lined up, the pieces fell into place, and I am eternally grateful.

4

THE HOMESTEADER

Those who look to read an orderly, linear account of my life experience may be disappointed, because I have chosen to pursue another path. The early history of migration from Europe and the settling of the Hoffman family in America follow a time line, and this I have related. Now, as the focus falls on my own nuclear family and on my own life, I have chosen to recall and write about events and experiences that are important to me and helped shape me into the person I am today. Such things may or may not be offered in chronological order. And so, I continue.

The salutation reads, "Dear Grandson Charles." This letter from my grandfather to me then proceeds to introduce an astounding incident that unfolded on the western plains of Canada in the year 1910. Prior to my receiving this letter, my grandfather Hoffman had told me his compelling story in person, and I knew at once that I would remember it the rest of my life. Nevertheless,

I asked him to put it into writing; I wanted to be certain that his tale would never be lost. His response to my request is dated November 30, 1960, and it came to me with its cover letter and five legal-sized pages of double-spaced, typewritten material. Needless to say, these are some of my most cherished possessions.

But before I share his story, let me tell you a little about the man, William Cyrus Hoffman. He was known to my brother and sister and me as Grandpa Hoffman. He was married for more than sixty years to our grandmother, Emily Blanche Snook. And while both of them were born in Pennsylvania, they met for the first time in the American West at a place called Rugby, North Dakota, the geographical center of North America that lies thirty-five miles south of the International Peace Garden between the United States and Canada. Grandma was nine years younger than Grandpa.

This is how it happened. Leaving Pennsylvania and traveling with her parents, my grandmother arrived in Rugby, North Dakota, in 1900. She was eleven years old. Then, three years later and traveling alone, my grandfather left Pennsylvania for the west and came to the same North Dakota town. At the time of their first meeting she was fifteen and he was twenty-four. And, although they did not know each other in Pennsylvania, it was not surprising that they would encounter each other out west. Rugby, located on the main line of the Great Northern Railway, was a frequent destination for Pennsylvanian Germans, so it housed a relatively large settlement of my grandparents' people.

I know nothing about their courtship, but they married in 1906 and settled in the Williston, North Dakota, area where my grandmother's parents had moved that same year. A year later the young couple confronted the tragedy of the twins' death and then, after another year, my uncle Clair was born, the oldest of the surviving children. Soon after Clair's birth William and Blanche and their little boy returned to Pennsylvania. But by the spring of 1910 they came back to the western part of the continent, this time settling across the international border as settlers in Canada.

At that time the Canadian government was offering land under the Dominion Lands Act, a piece of legislation modeled on the Homestead Act of the United States. Such land was available in the Canadian province of Saskatchewan, which was offering territory for hardy pioneers, men or women, who were willing to take over stewardship of a quarter section of virgin soil, 160 acres, and bring it into cultivation with cattle or crops. In those days they called it "proving up the land." This they had to do in order to gain legal ownership of the homestead.

The exact location of my grandparents' homestead can still be found in the historical land grant records of Saskatchewan: Part NW, Section 7, Township 03, Range 19, Meridian W 2. My grandparents and their growing family lived there for much of the period between 1910 and 1939, when they sold their hard-won property and moved to the west coast of Canada. But those twenty-nine years before the move to the Pacific Northwest were filled with activity other than proving up the land.

This was a period of his life when Grandpa's wanderlust was particularly acute. During that span of time the growing family was literally a moving target. In 1915 they shifted their living quarters from the sod house to a wooden-framed dwelling that Grandpa built on the homestead. The house had four rooms, two downstairs and two upstairs. The next summer they moved to Williston, North Dakota, where Grandma's parents were then living.

My aunt Jennie's comments on this relocation are telling. "Why Father made this move," she writes, "I do not know, but a pattern was emerging. Father could not seem to settle in any place for very long." As evidence of the fact, my grandfather, having secured employment with the Great Northern Railway, moved in 1917 to Havre, Montana.

The family had no choice but to follow the path of Grandpa's itchy feet. But once again, it was a brief stay. In 1918 he took his family back to Pennsylvania and to the small town of Muir where Grandpa worked as a carpenter in a coal mine. That year, 1918, marked the end of the First World War and the beginning of the worldwide influenza epidemic, which took many lives. And, although my grandparents' family was spared, Grandma became very sick and barely escaped with her life.

In spite of the problems, this was a sojourn my father always remembered as one of the happiest of his life. He was nine years old when they moved, but sadly for him, they moved back west in the spring of 1919. Grandpa simply packed up his family for yet another move and headed back to his farm in Saskatchewan. By that time, the family claimed the Canadian settlement of Gladmar as its hometown. Not long after the family's return to Canada, my grandfather was hired as the secretary-treasurer of the Surprise Valley Rural Municipality #9. And, somewhat unexpectedly, he held this position for sixteen years, from 1919 until 1935. Early in this period of time Grandma gave birth to another baby while Grandpa was away getting a wagonload of coal. Grandma was alone when the baby was born. I was told that she cut and tied the umbilical cord and then passed out.

By now there were six children in the family—Clair, Willard, Jennie, Norman, Ruth, and the new baby, Helen, made six. Three more children and the family would be complete. These three more were called Eldon, Annie, and Harold. Harold arrived in 1927, which means that Grandma birthed her eleven babies, including the twins who did not survive their first day, beginning when she was nineteen and ending when she was thirty-nine. During these years my grandfather remained on the move in spite of pregnancies, births, school, or whatever else impacted the family's life. But he always seemed to return to his demanding farm project on the homestead. It was a challenge he desperately wanted to conquer. But after heroic efforts to succeed, he at last gave up on the project and moved twelve hundred miles to the west coast of Canada and the city of Vancouver. By this time, 1939, most of the family had left home so Grandma and Grandpa departed the prairies with only three of the nine children who survived.

In later years my grandfather told his son, Eldon, he felt that he had been a failure in his attempt to be a farmer on the plains of Saskatchewan. What he may or may not have known is that the outcome was stacked against him. Writers of the North American West have pointed out that the problem with farming in this landscape was that there was not enough water. Wallace Stegner, one of the west's greatest authors, once wrote that "the primary unity of the West is a shortage of water." But the Homestead Act of the United States and the Dominion Lands Act of Canada both seemed to ignore this reality. And so it was that these farmers, after trying for years to get blood out of a stone, finally left their land. "Last one to leave the West turn out the lights" was their painful joke. Others, when they departed to return to former homes, were said to admit that "in God we trusted; in Kansas we busted." Many of those, as my grandfather, felt that they were failures.

But they were not failures. They were victims of a larger reality, Mother Nature. Nature allotted only so much moisture to this parched land and, unless a homesteader had many more acres than the government allowed he simply could not make it. Dreams dissolved like a mirage on the prairie. What makes this chapter of history even more tragic is that there were voices who pointed out that the quarter section or 160 acres was simply insufficient land for the farmer, and no one seemed to be listening. Unless the farmer could afford to purchase much more land than what was allotted, he was literally left out to dry.

But this gets me away from my story; there was plenty of excitement in those early years of the homestead that began in 1910. For me personally, the first few months of that enterprise were most important as it was during this time that my father was born. He was the second oldest of the surviving sons, born October 3, 1910. In the end, each of the nine children, four daughters and five sons, married and had children of their own.

As expected, there is a wealth of family stories that each of the siblings had to tell. One that always fascinated me concerns three of the family who married three siblings from another family. This makes the children of those pairings double cousins, and is even more interesting in the fact that this other family's surname was "Hoff." What happened is that three Hoffmans married three Hoffs. Helen Hoffman married a Hoff and so became Helen Hoff; Helen Hoff married a Hoffman and thus became Helen Hoffman. I'm not making this up. It's true.

Returning to my grandfather's homestead, I believe that it eventually amounted to a half section of land, 320 acres of opportunity, hardship, disappointments, and—in too many instances—defeat. The dimensions of the sod house where the family first lived were twenty by twenty-four feet. In places the walls were more than three feet thick. This is where the family would hunker down and survive the bitter cold and biting winds of the long northern plains winters.

That first year in the sod house winter came early. Grandpa's story begins late one early autumn afternoon when the falling snow and gusting wind threatened to become a full-fledged blizzard. Woe to anyone caught away from home and hearth on such a foreboding night. So it was not surprising to my grandparents when travelers on the trail from Weyburn, Saskatchewan, to Outlook, Montana, knocked on their door seeking refuge from the elements.

The young couple had no choice but to provide these wayfarers shelter in their already overcrowded dwelling.

But there was another visitor to the sod house who arrived in the fading light of that same day. Her name was Frances Behrenshausen. She was about twelve years old and she had become lost while she wandered the prairie looking for her father's cattle. My grandfather mentioned to me that she was not particularly well clad for the weather, a telling clue to the unrelenting poverty in which most of these people lived.

In those days the homesteads were open rangeland, and in most cases there were no fences. The cattle roamed freely over the landscape foraging for grass, and from time to time someone had to go out and bring them back to their barns. Now, with light fading, wind gusting, and snow blowing, someone was needed to take Frances home. If Frances did not return, then her own father might understandably wander into the winter wilderness looking for her and could easily perish in the quest to find his daughter. This would leave her an orphan as she had already lost her mother. So my grandfather decided he had to guide the girl home to her surviving parent.

In spite of the growing storm he was confident he could accomplish his self-assigned task. By his own admission, he considered himself a good plainsman, this tough five-foot-seven-inch, one-hundred-forty-pound carpenter who dreamed of a day when his homestead would be transformed into a proper farm such as he envisioned in his memories of Pennsylvania.

It was about half past three that afternoon when he put Frances on his horse and began leading the animal toward the Behrenshausen homestead some three and a half miles to the northwest. By four o'clock the combination of gathering storm and setting sun brought darkness to the little entourage of man, girl, and horse. Grandpa was pushing his luck; there were no visible landmarks, no lights nor visible stars, nothing to guide his steps in the vastness of this malevolent night. He had been to Frances's home only one time and he finally faced the reality that in the total blackness it would be easy to walk past the farm buildings and wander fatally into the freezing void.

So, groping in the darkness and realizing how easy it would be for him to miss his mark, he decided to change strategy. As a stockman he knew that a horse would find its way back to shelter and to its stablemates if it were given freedom to do so. They called it giving the animal its lead. So he handed the reins to Frances and carefully instructed her to let the horse pursue whatever direction it must take to find its way home. Under no conditions was she to put pressure on the reins and take the animal off course. So they set off. He now followed behind the horse and its rider and enjoyed the advantage of walking in the broken trail through the deepening snow. The horse led the way. But after a few miles he knew that his plan was not working. Unintentionally, Frances must have influenced the animal and so caused all three of them to be led astray. Grandpa was quite sure this is what had happened to turn the animal off its instinctive path to a safe haven, but there is no note of censure in his written account of what happened that fateful night.

Think about their predicament. My grandfather, then a young man who prided himself in his abilities as a man of the plains, was hopelessly lost in the blizzard. By now they had been hours wandering in this capricious storm. There had been lots of time for him to put his plight into focus. He was a husband and father trying to eke out a living for his loved ones on what might someday be a prosperous farm. There were no guarantees about that. Simply put, his life was a big gamble. He thought about his wife and his two sons sheltered in a house made out of prairie sod. One of the sons was a toddler, the other an infant. What would happen to them if he lost his life on this trail to nowhere that night? My grandfather was a man of his time and he considered it his primary responsibility to care for and protect his family. He needed to be there for them, and he agonized over the thought of leaving them to fend for themselves in this world that was forever demanding and endlessly difficult. Fashioning a life out of the raw material of a homestead was a most formidable task.

And then there was Frances, this young girl on the threshold of womanhood. Rather than setting out to take her home, he should have chosen the safety of his sod house for himself and for her as well. He should have waited out the storm in his rugged yet safe dwelling. She was his responsibility; she was young and had merely placed her trust in his wisdom and experience. Now he had jeopardized both of their lives. And the moment came when she begged him to let her surrender to the storm. She was too tired and too cold to go on. By now she had dismounted the horse and was walking with him in a desperate attempt to generate some heat and survive.

It was during this time, as she later recalled, that this man she knew as Mr. Hoffman took off his coat and gave it to her, rubbed her freezing hands and feet hoping to create some warmth, and finally knelt down in the snow to pray.

Many years later he told me how his foxhole prayer was answered. He said that the idea came to him to "walk into the wind"—to keep the wind hitting him always at the same angle so that, rather than walking in circles and getting nowhere, he and his charge would walk a straight line and hopefully arrive at a place of shelter. Clearly, it was a long shot but it turned out to be a sound decision.

They walked on. They struggled against the blizzard for what he said seemed like a great distance. Then, the horse stopped. It turned its head to the side and whinnied. The man and girl stopped in their tracks. They looked to see what the animal had sensed. And there it was. In a slight lull in the storm there appeared the faint outlines of a building. It turned out to be a vacant cabin and in that desperate moment it was too good to be true.

Making their way to the structure, Grandpa attempted to open the door. It was locked. He tried to open the window. It wouldn't budge. But he was a resourceful man. So, taking the horse to the lee side of the building where it would be sheltered from the icy wind, he searched his surroundings until he found a shovel. He could not have asked for a more appropriate discovery. Then, using the point of the shovel, he was able to shift the window and gain entrance to this answer to his prayers, this sanctuary from the unfriendly world that had held him in its menacing grip. Once inside, he found some matches, started a fire, and located an oil lamp, which illuminated the interior of the abandoned shack.

That night, said Frances, she went to sleep in the relative warmth of the cabin while Mr. Hoffman sat up and played solitaire as he waited for morning. At some point my grandfather found a clock and wound it so that he could reckon how long it took for the new day to break. Working from that point he reasoned that they had arrived at the shelter at 2:00 a.m., which means that for ten hours they had wandered hopelessly in that blizzard. My grandfather was not a big man physically. The night of the storm Frances did not have warm enough clothes and yet, for ten hours, these two had trudged and slogged their way through mile upon mile of the frozen landscape. The fact that the two of them were able to survive the ordeal is itself miraculous.

Morning dawned at last and brought with it the happy evidence that the storm had abated. And so, leaving Frances at the shack with strict instructions to stay there until his return, my grandfather was able to make his way to a neighboring farm, borrow a fresh horse, and finally reunite the girl with her family. He never told me, but I can imagine that, before leaving for the Behrenshausen homestead, he took care of his faithful horse until such time as he returned with Frances's father.

Strangely, in his account of the ordeal he says nothing about his reunion with his own family, with the two little boys, one my uncle and the other my father, and my grandmother, who had waited and wondered and worried and prayed that long night away.

I possess a letter, written with an unsure hand, that Frances Bell, née Behrenshausen, wrote to my parents when she herself was an elderly woman who had been left a widow by the death of her husband, Mike Bell. She speaks with affection of the memorable night a half century earlier when Mr. Hoffman brought her safely through the stormy ordeal. Over the years of her long life she had never forgotten the numbing cold, the freezing fear of that prairie nightmare, and the tenacity of Mr. Hoffman.

Although he never mentioned it to me, I believe my grandfather saw that dark night and its resolution as a metaphor of his entire life. At the time, he was thirty-one years old, still trying to find his way in the world. By his own admission, he was not only physically lost that memorable night, but he was adrift at the core of his being as well. This sense of disorientation is understandable; it was precipitated by the religious culture in which he was reared. Simply put, it meant that the fundamental issue in anyone's life is the person's relationship with the Almighty. With the absence of goodwill and conciliation at this juncture nothing else can be harmonized. Everything is out of kilter. This is the fixed point, the North Star, the cornerstone of it all. My grandfather knew this and accepted it intellectually, but he had not embraced it for himself. In fact, he was fighting against it. He makes this clear.

My grandfather saw himself as a lost soul. The storm without was reflected by the storm that raged in his own heart. And a moment of truth came when he finally knelt in the deepening snow to pray. He had exhausted all his options. He had come to the end of his resources as a proud homesteader. He even questioned whether he had the *right* to pray in the first place, to seek God's aid for the predicament in which he found himself. But pray he did, as people do in such extreme situations.

No matter how inhabitable the terrain, with its driven snow and biting wind and its impenetrable darkness, he could not get away from the unsettling reality at the center of his being. Yes, Frances was out there with him, and so was the horse for that matter. But something else or someone else was there, too.

There are those who would say that Mr. Hoffman's experience, his journey into his own wilderness, is common to the human condition. And I believe that it is true. Read the biography of Martin Luther, the man credited with initiating the so-called Protestant Reformation of the sixteenth century. His attention to fundamental matters of his own heart was brought about by his experience in a terrifying electrical storm. John Wesley, the Anglican priest whom I wrote about earlier, was brought to a place of personal reckoning through a storm at sea and the serene faith evidenced to him by a group of German Moravians who were his shipmates.

But many centuries earlier, before Wesley and Luther, an ancient poet probed this universal mystery of absence and presence, of being alone and of not being alone. So he queries the Almighty: "Where shall I flee from your presence?" The answer to this rhetorical question is that there is nowhere to flee. The answer means that not even a blinding storm on a vast plain in a forgotten corner of the earth can deny that inexplicable presence.

The English poet, Francis Thompson (1859–1907), continues to speak for many. In his most famous poem, "The Hound of Heaven," he describes his experiences as nothing less than the pursuit of his life by God. The poem expresses the poet's attempts to escape from the one who tracked him through his brief but largely miserable life. Understand, Francis Thompson led his pursuer on a formidable chase. Early in his life he fell into the clutches of opium addiction. He survived a lonely existence as a homeless man sleeping on the streets of London and on the banks of the River Thames. On one occasion he even tried to take his own life.

All of this and more he has in mind as he begins his 182 lines of poetry:

> I FLED Him, down the nights and down the days;
> I fled Him, down the arches of the years;
> I fled Him, down the labyrinthine ways
> Of my own mind; and in the mist of tears
> I hid from Him, and under running laughter.

There are some literary critics who would say that the greatest English writer of the twentieth century was an English journalist and essayist named Malcolm Muggeridge. Muggeridge's life spans most of the century, and his path through that period of time took him from socialism to communism to capitalism, none of which escaped the biting criticism of his skillful pen. He played an important role for the British and the rest of the Allied forces as he worked in the intelligence service during the Second World War. He was editor for a time of *Punch* magazine. Later in his life he became a Roman Catholic, spending considerable time championing the causes of people such as Mother Teresa of Calcutta and Aleksandr Solzhenitsyn of the former USSR.

At an earlier stage of his life, Muggeridge served as a teacher in India and it was during this time that he had opportunity to explore a little of the landscape in the extreme southwestern part of India. He tells of his solo forays into the Nilgiri Hills on horseback. From his vantage point in the mountains he marveled at the vistas of the valleys below him. In this fashion he spent days on the trails, usually in the company of himself alone. At least, during those travels he thought he was alone.

In his autobiography, Muggeridge describes his sense of being completely unaccompanied on his journeys. But he came to believe that it was more than a trip into the hills. It was a quest, a searching for something elusive, something he could not begin to describe. Then, in his reflections many years after the fact, he recalls how the impression came to him that not only was he questing for something, he was being pursued: "Footsteps padding behind me; a following shadow, a Hound of Heaven, so near that I could feel the warm breath on my neck."

From the journal he kept of his time in India, Malcolm Muggeridge reads faint pencil notes that pose the question: "Is this God?" Is it? The question is left hanging, unanswered, simply awaiting a response.

The question often waits, but not in my grandfather's case. He died in 1971 near Vancouver, where he had moved in 1939, the year of my birth. At the time of his death I was pastor of a small church nearby where his funeral was held. My cousin, Larry Hoff, and I were asked to preside at his funeral service. and we each felt greatly honored. As we closed that service we sang my grandfather's favorite hymn, the well-known, "O Love That Wilt Not Let Me Go." The words were penned by the nineteenth-century blind preacher, George Matheson. In the text, Matheson spoke of the faith of my grandfather as he affirmed his belief in a *light* that illumined and enlivened his every step, a *joy* that followed and encouraged him through every pain, and a *love*, deeper than the ocean, that would never stop pursuing him—a faith that shaped my grandfather's life over the course of ninety years.

5

THE CHRISTMAS BIBLE

My mother and father both grew up in the rural Canadian West in the early years of the twentieth century. They met one day when my father was out hunting coyotes. My mother's maiden name was Erma Agnes Sophia Carey. She and her younger brother, Ben, lived on the farm with her parents, Benjamin and Elizabeth Carey. This was a time when hardy pioneers were attempting to establish farms on both sides of the international border between Canada and its neighbor to the south. It was a tough assignment no matter which side of the border you were on, and many of these hopefuls failed to achieve the dream of making a living and raising a family off the land. If hard work alone could guarantee success, most of them would have made it. But there were too many uncontrollable factors, things such as availability of water, whims of weather, scarcity of funds, and incessant winds that turned dreams to dust.

Chet Huntley, the late NBC newscaster, was a contemporary of my parents. He was half of the *Huntley-Brinkley Report* that brought the evening news for many years on the network. Chet Huntley's childhood and formative years were lived on a farm in Montana, and I'm sure he shared many experiences my parents talked about as they remembered their past. Following retirement, Huntley wrote his memoirs in a slim volume entitled, *The Generous Years*. I'm sure he could have written that same book with a title that talked not only about the generous years, but also of the lean years, because those years were both lean and generous. They were generous in terms of human relationships, especially those within a family where members supported each other in the midst of shared hardships. I know that my father and his siblings always remembered what it was to be poor, not in terms of family and faith and love, but in the poverty of possessions and the means to wrest a living out of the unyielding land of a south Saskatchewan farm.

In my father's case, completing high school meant leaving home and moving to one of the larger towns where there was enough revenue to support a high school. But it would cost more than his parents could afford, so any aspirations for a high school diploma were out of the question. This was the reality of life during his teen years in the 1920s, 1923 being the year he turned thirteen. And it was followed by the privations of the Great Depression during the 1930s.

My parents married in 1933, the middle of that depressed decade. That year Mother would turn eighteen and Father would mark his twenty-third birthday. I have no doubt that they were deeply in love with each other, but employment for either of them was virtually nonexistent, so they faced a huge hurdle.

At some point in the 1930s, the price of gold doubled in value from sixteen dollars per ounce to thirty-three dollars per ounce. So, when my father read in a magazine that there was still gold to be found in the interior of British Columbia, it got his attention. One thing led to another and, before long, he and two of his friends drove their Model T Ford car to a town called Barkerville near the headwaters of the Fraser River. Predictably, the old car broke down along the way and they found themselves stranded outside the town of Lethbridge in southern Alberta. Needing a part for the Model T, two of the men set out walking on a railroad bridge that spanned a deep gorge but was a shortcut to the town. Once there they would purchase the needed part while Father stayed with the car. The story he told about his two comrades, however, was a chiller. While the two were on the bridge a train passed, forcing them to seek safety by hanging over the edge of the structure three hundred feet above the ground.

Eventually, they all made their way to Barkerville only to learn that there was no viable employment in the gold industry. The time had come for them to improvise, the improvisation taking the form of a sluice box on the Fraser River near the town of Quesnel. Throughout that summer of 1934 they shoveled gravel into the water-washed sluice and isolated the gold. Apparently, they retrieved enough of the precious metal to subsist. Mother, who had been staying with her family in Saskatchewan, then made her way west by train to join her husband. That fall my mother and father built a log cabin into which they hunkered down for the long, cold winter of 1934 and 1935.

"That was the longest winter of my life," Father told me thirty-five years later. The two of us were on our way to the site where his old log cabin once stood as a challenge to the Great Depression and the northern winter. Amazingly, we found what was left of the structure. It was falling down, a victim of time and neglect. But enough of it was there so that he could collect a few pieces of intact logs from which he fashioned miniatures of the original cabin for his children and grandchildren.

Today, I cherish my little cabin, remember the journey that I took with my dad, and rejoice that he had this one great adventure, the details of which remained in his memory the rest of his life.

During all of his formative years my father, as most of his generation, faced formidable odds. The Hungry Thirties, a name coined to denote the great economic depression of that decade, were followed by the Second World War of the 1940s. My father never recovered from these so-called accidents of history that robbed him of the formal education he knew he needed. He made his way through life feeling ill prepared to assume his rightful place in the order of things. For him, it was a burden that never lifted; his lack of formal education weighed heavily upon him and left him with a crippling inferiority complex.

One consequence of Father's lack of formal education was the fact that our home, the one I grew up in, lacked a certain degree of sophistication and of intellectual stimulation. We did not know, for example, how to go about pursuing education in our formative years and then over the course of our lives. We did not understand how exposure to the arts and sciences could enhance our lives; how knowledge of history and literature was worth knowing even if only for its intrinsic value.

I do not blame my parents for this shortfall in the culture of our home. I understand how it came about and I am happy to say that we were saved by our mother's optimism, our father's humor, even the dark variety, and the expressions of love that we felt from each of them. Still, there was not a lot of intellectual freedom in our home. New ideas and original thinking had to compete with entrenched dogma administered from the top down. I chuckle at the memory now, but I recall occasions when conversation at the supper table became too lively and a little uncomfortable for my dad. So he put an end to it. "Pipe down and eat!" he would pontificate. Listening to all sides of an argument was not one of his strong suits. During the ensuing silence my brother and sister and I would quietly finish our meal as we stole furtive glances at one another and exchanged knowing smiles. I suppose most children do the same thing as they try to enlighten their parents.

I note this characteristic of my father with no intention of diminishing him. My father was clever and smart, and I respected him. Now, all these years later, I know that I loved him then and love him still. I remember him with affection, recalling his ability to see the comic side of life, and remembering how much I enjoyed listening to his stories. He would regale us with his dry wit and his unique way of phrasing descriptions. He was a natural and gifted raconteur. He loved to amuse people with his tales.

Something else I will never forget about my father was his unflagging commitment to his family, his friends, and his faith. He was indeed a man whose word was his bond. He was scrupulously honest. In fact, my maternal step-grandfather, a bit of a rogue himself, would often castigate Father for his tenacious commitment to honesty and truth. Grandfather was originally from Switzerland where he had learned to speak German, French, and Italian. Added to that was his thickly accented English. "Villard," he would say, "you can't be too honest." My dad, whose name was Willard, would smile and say, "That's right, Donald, you can't be too honest." The statement worked for both of them, although they each took it in a different way.

Father has been gone for many years and I am nearing the age he was when he died. But the wonderful thing is that I know and understand him better now than I ever did before. Time will do that for us if we allow it, if we open ourselves to its refining and reshaping influences, and if we offer it the same sort of grace that has been given to us.

Having shared some of my childhood history, you will not be surprised when I tell you that there were relatively few books and magazines in our home. We did have a set of encyclopedias, a daily newspaper, the Holy Bible, and various small pamphlets and booklets on relatively unimportant religious topics. Our shelves were essentially devoid of the classics of English literature.

A literary highlight for us was the arrival of the mail-order catalog. Here was a photographic cornucopia of everything from underwear to hardware, games to guns, and whatever else that was required to maintain the average home. This catalog of goods came twice a year in two different editions: the fall and winter edition followed by the spring and summer. Frequently, my parents used the fall and winter version for their Christmas shopping. Whenever that happened the gifts were of a practical nature, and the problem was that catalog clothing looked much better in the slick photographs of models than it did on the growing child.

Once, when my parents deviated from the boys clothing department and ordered me a Bible for Christmas, complete with my name embossed on the cover in gold letters, I was devastated. Eleven-year-old boys are not excited by Bibles as Christmas gifts. Worse yet, I knew that I would have to face the inevitable question from my friends: "Hey, Charlie, what did you get for Christmas?" I remember my answer: "I got a book." I vowed to myself that I would not reveal the specifics. That was my response, a reply I rehearsed in order to be ready when the inevitable question arose.

To most of my friends, a Bible for Christmas would be as welcome as a *mess of pottage*, not that any of them would have the faintest idea what a mess of pottage was. None of them even attended church, let alone understood it. So they could not be expected to comprehend why anyone their age would go there four times a week. But I coveted their acceptance and this well-intentioned Christmas gift did nothing to further my cause and dispel my pals' misconceptions about who I was.

The Christmas Bible was a challenge; it was also a metaphor for much of my life. As it turned out, our family was eminently countercultural many years before any of us had ever heard the term. For us, Sunday was a day of rest, our Sabbath, in actual fact the day we exhausted ourselves with trips to the church for Sunday school, morning worship, and evening service. As the world around us donned their casual attire to embark on games, picnics, and an endless variety of outings, we put on our uncomfortable Sunday suits and headed for church. As a child who loved the outdoors in every sort of weather, this was not a requirement I enjoyed. In fact, I remember to this day how good it felt to shed the Sunday uniform and settle into my everyday clothes.

Church for us was concerned not so much with the towering Hebrew Decalogue, the Ten Commandments, nor with the great Hebrew and Christian law of love as Jesus restated it. Church came with a lot of baggage. Church burdened us with prohibitions, many of which were loosely tied to our Bibles, and effectively tied us in knots before sending us out to contend with a secular world. Too often we were diminished by our faith rather than enlarged by it. For us, everything was black and white; there were no subtle shades of meaning. We were afraid to admit uncertainty and extremely uncomfortable with the nuances that are an inevitable part of life. We had a great fear of making a mistake, of letting the side down or, perish the thought, of letting God down. We needed to know the answers and we needed to be absolutely sure that we were right.

Personally, this sharp dichotomy between the culture of the church and the culture of the larger society left me in a constant state of uneasiness, a condition especially and acutely painful during the years of my high school career. Consider how it was. Sundays began with popular radio preacher Charles E. Fuller and his long-running radio program called *The Old Fashioned Revival Hour*, followed by the congregational hymn "Holy, Holy, Holy," which we sang from the pages of our hymnals at church. Mondays, by contrast, were invoked with Nat King Cole crooning about "the lazy hazy days of summer" and Elvis warning the world to stay off his blue suede shoes.

I think I can honestly say that during those confusing days I loved Jesus but I wasn't sure about some of his friends. Years later I came across a description of those self-styled holy folk as Christians in the worst sense of the word. Yes, there were exceptions; not everyone wore their faith like the proverbial hair shirt. Thank God, there were those whose faith was winsomely woven into the material of life, people who lived with integrity and without guile. There were people of the church who were possessed by a vitality that evidenced itself in the various facets of their living. But they were in the minority. And in my case their voices were dim; I heard them only faintly because the doomsday folks had the floor.

For me, the religious climate of home and church was overwhelming. I was a sensitive child for whom it was impossible to break rules with impunity. And I craved acceptance. Mother, Father, teachers, pastors, and especially God: I was crippled if I did not have their blessings. Minor infractions against what I perceived as the laws of God weighed me down, and as I entered my teen years my conflicted life had become a load too heavy to carry.

It is not as though there was no joy in my life; there was, lots of it. I was blessed in so many ways. I was secure in my family, at least to a point. In my own mind I thought that if they knew the real me things might be different. Nevertheless, I had a large extended family who took notice of me: grandparents on both sides, cousins my own age, interesting and sometimes eccentric uncles and aunts, even ancient and distant *greats*. My father had four brothers and four sisters and most of them, along with their spouses and children, lived in our area. The big difference was that we were the only ones who lived in the country; we were the country bumpkins and they were the city slickers. We had ten acres of land; they lived in small houses on tiny city lots. So ours was the destination of the city dwellers who would often pay us a visit on Saturdays or Sundays. We had no telephone so we seldom knew when they were coming. They just showed up. It must have been a challenge for my mother to fix the meals with no notice, but they kept coming. And that's how I formed special relationships with a long list of kinfolk. In the summer my cousins would sometimes spend a week with us on the farm—happy days.

But besides all this, I enjoyed the company of friends who lived within walking or cycling distance of my home. Together, in what I now know as pristine years, the halcyon days, we fished the small streams that coursed through our ranging playground, soared over canyons and creeks on one-rope swings, learned to swim in the Pacific Ocean, floated makeshift rafts in ponds and streams, climbed high in the branches of trees to see our world from another vantage point, and when the season was right we gorged ourselves on fresh cherries or plums or strawberries. We played pickup games of softball, not because our parents had enrolled us for a team, but because it was the thing *we* wanted to do. We kicked soccer balls endlessly and in every kind of weather. One time we built hammocks out of gunnysacks, hung them in the woods, and slept there until the rain chased us to a nearby barn where we spent the rest of the night nestled in the hay. One time we dammed up three channels of a small creek to create a pool that was deep enough to swim in. Winter would find us skating on a pond under a starry night and a full moon. When the snow was right we built bobsleds, jumped on, and sped down the slopes.

A gentle path winding its way through the woods is a favorite memory. Bordering the path would be ferns and bracken that carpeted the forest floor in the filtered light. Next were the alder and birch trees and the occasional vine maple standing as first watch over the narrow footpath that gave us access to our woods. From the gnarled vine maple we would cut v-shaped crutches with which we would fashion our slingshots to catapult stones at whatever targets challenged us. And as backdrop to all of this were the great denizens of the forest—the cedar, the hemlock, the Sitka spruce, the Douglas fir—all the majestic evergreens that were there long before any of us walked the earth and, unless they were harvested for lumber and paper products, would be there long after we were gone. If it were late spring or summer when we walked the path we might see the happy dogwood blossoms, the floral emblem of British Columbia, with a range that carried them southward to central California. And there were wild berries, too. They delighted our foray into the woods—delicate huckleberries, red thimbleberries, along with red and orange salmonberries; all of them irresistible. I loved to walk the nave of that open-air cathedral.

Even now, the memories excite me. But as full of wonder and romance all of that was, the night would always come, I would lay my head on the pillow, and I would have to pay the piper. No one deserved such unaccountable, innocent pleasure. That's how I felt; that is what I thought in those lonely moments. No one, especially I, deserved it.

It all came to a crisis for me during the last days of my senior year of high school. It had begun as a small, insignificant infraction against the *Great Rule Book* when I was twelve years old and in the eighth grade. A classmate and I had gotten into trouble over some small incident, I cannot recall what it was, and were told to report to the teacher at the end of the school day. My friend told the teacher a lie, which served to get us off the hook. And I, aged twelve, caught off guard and finding myself in a moral dilemma, ended up protecting my friend by playing along with the untruth. From that moment that incident plagued my conscience endlessly. Guilt was my constant companion for a period of nearly five years, and by the time I was a senior in high school I was a full-fledged insomniac.

At times, I would lie awake all night. I remember hearing the birds begin to sing their welcome to a new day, and I had not yet slept. I remember the panic I felt as the dawn quietly filled my bedroom with its light. Soon I would need to be up and off to school, and I had not slept.

Most people I know cannot begin to relate to such an experience of juvenile paranoia, and for this I am glad. But as I reflect on those dark days I am aware that unexamined, fear-based, authoritarian religion still flourishes in our culture. It is parceled out every Sunday from many pulpits of the land, and it is nurtured in some of our homes. And while it may work in some cases, I believe its overall effect diminishes those who live under its spell, and that it distorts their notion of God. For such people grace is measured. They tend to dwell on the fringes of life, to keep score, and to complain that the party, which ought not to have been planned in the first place, is seriously out of control.

It was June of 1956; it was the evening before my high school graduation. Celebrations were planned and they included driving to Vancouver's Chinatown for a midnight dinner and staying up all night to mark this milestone of our education. As I went to bed I reminded myself of the obvious—I needed a good night's sleep. That reminder was the so-called kiss of death; I tossed and turned as the old demon guilt danced his way into control. I don't know, but I suppose I was a little like the biblical Jacob wrestling with the angel. He lost, too.

At some point during those long hours I got out of bed, walked into my parents' bedroom, and said, "I need help." My mother and father listened as I attempted to tell them what my life really looked like, that I was riddled with guilt, and that I was not the saint they thought me to be. Mother and Dad were both stunned to hear these things but they listened well. And when the moment was right, my father directed my thinking to some appropriate parts of the Bible, the same book that had given me so much grief that Christmas of my eleventh year. He helped me see that the grace of God meant that I no longer needed to shoulder this dreadful and pathetic burden, this all-consuming guilt that had turned the past one-third of my young life into a nightmare. I am still thankful to him for his sensitivity and wisdom in helping me that night.

As a lifelong student of the Bible, I know that the writings yield mixed messages—often our own fault rather than the Bible's. Nowhere does the sacred text suggest that we worship the Bible. And when readers get caught in such bibliolatry they find themselves in any number of quandaries. Resulting in part from this, different people stress different aspects of what their sacred texts have to say. Some people lay emphasis on the laws of God, others on the grace of God. That's one example, and my dad tended to come down on the side of law and judgment. But not that night. That night he knew what his son needed to hear. More than anything else, he needed to hear a word of forgiveness and grace and hope and assurance—assurance that the past could be left behind and that he could move forward into a promising future.

I now know that, important as that nocturnal experience was, it was not the end; it was only a start, admittedly an essential beginning. Since that day, a long journey has ensued for me. There have been sidesteps and backtracks, stumbling one moment and soaring another, some successes and many failures. I have had to come to terms with new experiences and new information as I have made my way through a lifetime. The world is not the same as it was in 1956, and I am certainly not the same. But listen to this: the essence of what took place in the wee hours of that encounter when my father introduced me to a God of grace is still with me. That has not changed.

I did not get much sleep the rest of that night. I learned that guilt wasn't the only thing that could hold sleep at bay. Joyful relief could do it, too, and it did. I am forever grateful.

6

THE CHICKENHOUSE CHURCH

In the sixteenth century of the Christian church a group of people who became known as Protestants broke with the people known as Roman Catholics and then went on to break with each other *ad infinitum.*

Such wholesale division where there should have been unity is seen by many as scandalous—a betrayal of the essence of the church. But it has continued for more than five hundred years and the result is an endless list of denominations that labor under the banner of Protestantism. In the early years of my life I passed through a number of these Protestant churches.

My mother was raised as a nominal Roman Catholic, the daughter of an Anglican mother and a Catholic father. My father grew up in a strict, black-and-white, hard-line Protestant tradition. When the two of them married in 1933, they settled on being Protestants because my father would have it no other way and, in my mother's case, I suspect that love trumped church loyalties. It often happens that way.

Churches of my youth were chosen according to their proximity to where we lived during those years. The first that I remember was of the Baptist variety and was located in the small city of Prince Albert in northern Saskatchewan. Saskatchewan is directly north of North Dakota and Montana. Prince Albert, in the north, took its name from Queen Victoria's late husband, Albert, who died in 1861 at the age of forty-two. We moved to Prince Albert on the day of my second birthday, October 7, 1941, and left two months before my fourth birthday. It was a brief stay, perhaps abbreviated by the fact that the winters were brutal—while there we experienced temperatures reaching to sixty degrees Fahrenheit below zero. Nevertheless, I have lasting memories of my young life there. It was there, for instance, that I had my first haircut, long overdue but most welcome because until then I wore ringlets. Apparently, my mother thought my hair was too beautiful to cut and, besides, I was supposed to be a girl in the first place. My parents wanted a girl to go along with the boy they already had. So, as I went through those early years I was constantly being mistaken for a girl. Whether this ordeal during my first two years left any lasting marks on my self-image I cannot say. I know I was happy for that haircut, because it said clearly that I was a boy. And boys *will* be boys.

In another memory from those early years I see myself standing with my mother as we watched Canadian soldiers marching down the main street of Prince Albert and presumably off to Europe and the grim task of fighting in the Second World War. Through the eyes of a three-year-old child, it was a splendid and romantic sight, but now I wonder how many of those young men suffered and died in Europe never to return to their "home and native land" when the war finally ended in 1945. Many others went through the rest of their lives carrying physical and emotional scars.

My generation owes more than it can ever repay to those young men who fought the Second World War and thereby preserved freedom for so many millions of people in the world today. Some of us remember the sentiment expressed by the poet John McCrae when he wrote about the Flanders Fields in Belgium and particularly about the servicemen who died in the war and were laid to rest in its cemetery. McCrae speaks as one of the fallen and this is what he says:

> If ye break faith with us who die
> We shall not sleep, though poppies grow
> in Flanders fields.

Given the historical moment and the field of ultimate sacrifice, keeping the faith with those who made such a sacrifice is a noble and most appropriate goal. McCrae wrote his poem with reference to the men who died in the First World War, but they are apropos to the Second as well, and I believe that our grade-school teacher was justified in having us memorize McCrae's words.

Still, the more I learn about war and all of its complex ramifications the more I abhor it. The year of my birth, 1939, marked the beginning of the Second World War for Great Britain and its commonwealth of nations. So I was too young for that campaign and the same for the battles of the Korean Peninsula. When Vietnam came along I was a divinity school student living temporarily in the United States and, although I had to register with the selective service, I was classified so far down the list of possible inductees that there was little chance of my being conscripted. So I have not experienced war firsthand. I do know that the decision as to whether to go to war is never easy to determine. History suggests that there are pros and cons on both sides and each side has its supporters. I do believe that monsters such as Adolf Hitler must not be allowed to work their sinister mischief in the world. And if such a leader's own people cannot stop him, then others must.

I have little patience with those who would go to war willy-nilly, which I have seen during the course of my life. What do these people think? Families are torn apart, limbs are severed from bodies, minds are concussed, psyches destroyed, death is everywhere and never so grotesque—and this is acceptable? I cannot believe it. And then there is the feeble attempt by some to assuage their guilt by broadcasting the word that we must support our troops, that these are our heroes. Underlying this is a facile understanding of patriotism. It is sadly true. As always, humanity's ability to heal its wounds lags far behind its ability to inflict those wounds in the first place. None of this did I know as a child of three years old watching young men go off to war. In childish innocence I stood by the main street in Prince Albert and witnessed those young men marching to an unknown future, and into many instances a future that was cut off much too early.

Prince Albert was the place where, after being confronted by what seemed like the biggest dog in the world, I adopted my lifelong skittishness toward the canine species. It was also where, at the age of three years, I launched a brief life of crime when I lifted a toy from one of the store shelves, slipped away from my parents, and walked home to show off my ill-gotten loot to my brother and his friends. It didn't work. My parents were quick to find me at the sandbox with my brother, instantly figured out what had happened, and marched me back to the store to return the hot goods and apologize to the store owner. Many years later, as a member of a college choir, I visited the jail in Prince Albert with a singing group that I was part of and performed for the inmates. Fortunately, I was on the right side of the bars, although a case could be made that my singing alone would have been cause enough for my incarceration.

I was telling you about the Baptist church and Sunday school—I have no memory of my parents ever attending services there, only a faint recollection of the fact that I was one of its Sunday school scholars.

The next stop in my journey through Protestantism was in British Columbia's Fraser River Valley where our family settled in 1943 after leaving the frigid city of Prince Albert and where my sister Lorraine was born soon after our arrival. We attended a very small Church of the Nazarene that was located, believe it or not, on Jericho Road. There I remember listening to a man who offered very long and very loud prayers, as though God was not only hard of hearing but a long way off. One Sunday, a whole family got up and left in the middle of his raging imprecations; they never returned. Later, when the church decided to build a new sanctuary, the congregation temporarily had no place to meet so my father offered them a room in our chicken house. I'm not making this up. I don't know how many people went searching for another church under those conditions or how long the church met there or if they installed a piano to accompany congregational singing in the chicken house church. But one of the songs I remember hearing was titled, "When the Saints Go Marching In." A line I recall from the piece expressed the prayer, "Lord, I want to be in that number when the saints go marching in." That seemed to be a favorite, although I saw nothing in my limited experience of churches to commend its sentiment. I have since wondered if our neighbors knew that our henhouse had become a church or if they merely thought we had unusually talented chickens.

The next stop on my tour of Protestantism was an Anglican Sunday school that my brother and I attended sporadically after yet another move. I remember it as a small wooden structure with white siding. It was located on the southeast corner at the intersection of Otter Road and the Trans Canada Highway. It was here that I was introduced for the first time to the Apostles' Creed with its, "I believe in the Holy Spirit, the holy catholic church," a source of confusion for the two Hoffman boys who had been informally catechized into believing that the Roman Catholic Church was one of the world's great evils. Happily, I learned later in life that the creed was referring to the *universal* church and not restricted to the *Roman Catholic Church* with its center in Rome and its divine leader, the

Pope. To this day I continue to recite the creed wherever it is used in worship.

This particular move was temporary, a house rented for twenty-five dollars per month on Otter Road, a reminder of earlier times when otters lived in the small stream that made its way through our small world. There we lived while Father, with the rest of his family as the construction crew, built a modest three-bedroom bungalow into which we moved in 1949. From time to time my father's friends would show up to lend a hand, and skilled help came from my grandfather, William Cyrus Hoffman, who was a superb craftsman and experienced carpenter. By that time Grandma and Grandpa had settled into their home at 949 East 14th Avenue in the city of Vancouver.

Father labored valiantly to build that house on what was then called Latimer Road in the municipality of Surrey in British Columbia. He had an eight-to-five job Monday through Friday in a store that sold animal feed and farm supplies, so his work on the house was done in the evenings and on weekends and holidays. Still, when we finally occupied the house in the late summer of 1949, the building was far from completed. We had no central heating, no running water, and no well for water supply. Actually, I do not know where our water came from during that time. But my father had obviously found a source from which he hauled the precious liquid to our home in his Model A Ford.

I recall that he set himself to the task of digging a well beneath our dirt-floored basement. As the hole deepened it reached a place where Mother's assistance was needed.

He, down in the well hole, would fill a bucket with soil and she, with the help of a winch, would crank the bucket and its contents to the surface, empty it, and then send it back to the bottom of the hole where Father would refill it. As the well inched its way downward my father had installed what is called cribbing, a wooden lining of the square walls to prevent the dirt from collapsing and trapping him below. Mother and Father stayed with the task until they finally struck water some twenty feet under the basement floor. But it wasn't what they hoped for. It turned out that the water was not potable; it was bitter, had a foul odor, and we were afraid to use it.

Eventually Dad found a solution to our predicament. Our next-door neighbor had successfully employed professionals to drill for water. So my father worked out a deal where he would purchase, install, and maintain the pumping equipment needed to get the water not only to the neighbor's house, but to ours as well. There was plenty of water, the pump was well maintained, and everyone was happy with the arrangement.

But we still had a long list of challenges to face on the way to making that house a comfortable dwelling. For example, the partitions between the rooms were incomplete. The studs were in place but there was no drywall. So, with the exception of our parents' enclosed bedroom, you could see into one room from the next. Also, there was no bathroom and the outside walls were covered with black tar paper. I suppose part of my salvation as far as saving face with my friends was the fact that a lot of other people lived under similar Spartan conditions in those days following the

Second World War when the first of the generation called baby boomers were arriving on the scene.

In spite of all the drawbacks, this house, more than any of the others, was our childhood home. Certainly it is the home that I remember with the greatest fondness. I'm not sure that it was ever completed but over time it was greatly improved and, for better or worse, it was ours and we loved living there. Into that home we invited our friends and occasionally held parties for our church youth group. For some of our friends it became a second home. Sadly, the house with all the precious memories is gone now, a victim of progress torn down to make room for modern condominiums. Even the address has changed, Latimer Road is now known as 192nd Street.

It was here also that we finally found a church home. This one identified itself as the Evangelical Free Church. In reality its beliefs were much like those of the conservative Baptists or Methodists, but in this case most of the active members were former German Mennonites, another bit of fallout from the Protestant Reformation. So a lot of German language was spoken, especially by parents of my friends and other older folks. You might say that we were an English-speaking congregation with a fondness for sauerkraut. Here our family got involved. Our parents became members, taught Sunday school, attended virtually whenever the lights were on, gave liberally of their finances, befriended the pastors, entertained guest speakers, transported members who needed a ride to church events, and served on boards and committees. For many years my father was the trustworthy and meticulous church treasurer. No one could have been more conscientious and diligent for the task.

On the lighter side of things, I remember that from time to time the pastor would surrender the Sunday evening service to the laity. They called it Christian Endeavor and it was an evening not to be missed. These were the days before television had taken over Sunday evenings and for us this was the only show in town.

I have since learned that yielding a church service to the machinations of the laity is one of the greatest acts of faith imaginable, especially at that place. People stepped forward to read scripture, recite poems, sing songs, and play instruments. I remember that once or twice my father was asked to deliver the sermon. That was the one area where the pastor exercised leadership so that things did not unravel completely.

The highlight of all the evenings of Christian Endeavor foisted upon that congregation was the Mix family instrumentalists. I seem to recall Father referring to them as the "Mixed-Up Family." How many of them there were I cannot say, but each one had an instrument. The intonation for these instruments was never harmonized; it was always off, a glorious disharmony, with the result that none of the musical instruments was in tune with the next. The leader was Mr. Mix and his trumpet. Have you ever seen a man with no teeth playing the trumpet? Well, I have and I can tell you, you don't forget a thing like that. God bless Mr. and Mrs. Mix and all the little Mixes. Their music might have made the older folks cry but my generation eagerly looked forward to whatever they had to offer. Without them

I probably would have no memory of those Sunday evenings known as Christian Endeavor at the church.

I must report that, while we were busy finding our way to the Celestial City with help from these Evangelical Free Church people, my father's youngest brother, Harold, was busy leading a Church of the Nazarene congregation not far away. When it came to the pastoral duties in a small church, my uncle Harold was a triple threat. Not only did he preach sermons, he also played the piano and sang songs. Occasionally we would visit his church on a Sunday evening, enjoying and taking part in the zesty congregational singing. Harold had attended a Canadian college operated by the Church of the Nazarene. He seemed to enjoy his time at that school and I found myself getting caught up in his enthusiasm. So it was that after considering some other alternatives I decided to follow in his footsteps and enroll at the same place.

At some point during those four years of college I made the decision to join the Church of the Nazarene, the first time I had ever formally aligned myself with a particular Protestant denomination. And thus began a decade and a half of my association with one of the so-called *holiness* churches. By this time I not only knew about the ecumenical movement, I *was* the ecumenical movement, with involvement in no less than four separate Protestant denominations by the time I was a teenager.

As time went by I grew restless in my chosen church home and began looking for another. Granted, it was there I had received my college and seminary education, there I ended up teaching at the church's Canadian college for six years, and there I had given leadership as pastor to a local church for what was a brief two years but felt more like a decade. It was not a good fit for me, and my own sense of integrity demanded that I find another setting for my life.

There is nothing unusual about this experience; it happens frequently. In many instances people simply give up on the church scene, perhaps hold on to a modicum of faith, and look forward to weekends with no commitments. I understand that, but for me it was not an option. I needed a replacement. While it sometimes felt as though the church was doing its best to send me packing, I held my ground. I was the pesky lint on a blue blazer; I wouldn't let go. Eventually, I'm happy to say, I found a place of refuge and challenge in another Protestant denomination within the broad landscape of my religious tradition.

This new denomination, the United Methodist Church, does not exist in Canada but is centered in the United States. Is it or was it ever perfect? Of course not; there is always room for improvement and plenty of reason for criticism. But for me the air is more refreshing, the atmosphere is more hospitable, and the problems easier to live with. I never expected perfection and I got what I expected.

Human exiles will offer plenty of reasons for their status, and I have done this, too, often ungraciously, when talking with others about my own sectarian departure. The challenge when speaking about this sort of thing is to be aware of the larger issues that usually underlie the situation. In my case it was a sense of confinement to a world that was too small. It seemed that my world was much larger than my church wanted to admit. What was a source of great comfort to some of my friends was stifling to me. I never cultivated that feeling; it just turned out that way.

I am a faithful believer in what we call transcendence, but not to the exclusion of the sensory world in which we live. The world I left behind pushed this idea of otherworldliness too far for me. In the end it felt like a sort of ghetto with its own traditions, rules, rubrics, and sacred cows. In my case, the list of accepted beliefs and behaviors was too small for the world I knew and in which I lived. This was my experience, one that resulted in my decision to move to another venue for myself and my family. It was not an easy decision, but both then and now I believe it was the right choice.

Many of the people I knew, including cherished friends and relatives, stayed with their church and contributed to its life and calling. They supported it with their giving, attended worship regularly, sent their children to summer camps, involved themselves in missionary activities, saw their youth off to the church's colleges, and opened their homes to each other. They stayed for the simple reasons that they found within their church's borders a depth of fellowship, a sense of belonging, a promise of the hereafter, and a measure of purpose that was lacking in so much of twentieth-century life. The church provided a safe haven as people passed through the twentieth century's turbulence of two world wars, the Korean conflict, the unsettling war in Vietnam, a great economic depression, the upheavals of the 1960s, and all that followed from that period's iconoclastic spirit.

I have always believed that what we think or what we teach about our faith ought to be readily accessible. It should resonate with our most honest human feelings and experiences. My wonderfully wise father-in-law, Trevor Morgan, was fond of saying that the fundamental truths of God and of life are both simple and profound. He was right. And I believe that divine lessons taught in the classroom of humanity must be capable of enlightening the simplest mind while challenging the most intellectual talent. And when it is at its best, the church speaks to and has room at one and the same time for people such as the humble cook known as Brother Lawrence along with the brilliant twentieth-century theologian named Karl Barth. In the church the char woman and the big steeple pastor come together at the same table of Holy Communion. Such is the power and the grace of the Christian gospel and such ought to be the beauty of the church.

Years ago I came across profound yet simple writings from the nineteenth-century French novelist Gustave Flaubert. In a short story entitled "A Simple Heart," he tells of a humble woman called Félicité whose faith is grounded in the most common, everyday experiences of her life. One day she takes the children under her care to their confirmation class. As Félicité waits for them she fixes her eyes on the plain stories portrayed in the stained glass windows of the church. And, as her priest relates the Bible's sacred history to the confirmation class, Félicité is moved to tears. "Then," says Flaubert, "she wept at the story of the Passion. Why had they crucified Him, when He loved the children, fed the multitudes, healed the blind, and had willed, in His meekness, to be born among the poor, on the dung heap of a stable? The sowings, harvests, wine-presses, all the familiar things the Gospel speaks of, were part of her life. They had been made holy by God's passing; and she loved the lambs more tenderly for love of the Lamb, and the doves because of the Holy Ghost."

Christianity's deepest meanings are that accessible. And so it was that a time came in my life when I was no longer comfortable with the teaching of my particular corner of the "holy catholic church." And while I loved and still love many of its people, I had to move on to something else. Like my eighteenth-century ancestor, I had to immigrate from a place that was no longer viable for me and to seek a new land where I could live out my faith—a theme to which I shall return.

As is true for most, my four years of college set much of the course of my life. Sadly, I have to admit that college was not as enriching an intellectual experience as it should have been. I take responsibility for this. I was an immature student in just about every way. I cut corners, missed assignments, and got by. I survived by being clever but I did not take advantage of the opportunity to enhance my understanding of life, to augment my superficial knowledge of the world, to broaden my point of view, or to deepen my insight into the ways of the world. I am not proud of this. In fact, even in my retirement I am painfully aware that I made irreversible mistakes at that important period.

This does not mean that good things did not come out of that time. During those years I enjoyed a comfortable community of persons who were like-minded in many ways, an extended family in which I was accepted and appreciated and given opportunities to exercise modest leadership skills. I was introduced to new forms of music and began to embrace the rich heritage of music's sacred tradition. I never came near being a musician but I had many chances to participate in choirs and small ensembles and, by watching others, I came to appreciate the talent and discipline required truly to become proficient in any chosen field. At that little college, with all of its flaws and shortcomings, I deepened my respect for the art of preaching, an unexamined belief that I brought with me when I first enrolled there but one that I carry with me still. And now, looking back over half a century, I am sure that it was there that I began my lifelong journey toward an understanding of the human condition with all of its complexities.

As important as anything that I garnered from college are the friendships that to this day continue to enrich my life. Some of us old college friends get together from time to time, and when we do it's as though we have never been apart; we simply pick up where we left off the last time we met. We know each other so well that there is no room for airs, no place for duplicity, no point in overstating our achievements, and no reservations that would prevent us from celebrating each other's successes. This is the essence of friendship that is worthy of the name.

Halfway through the last year of college my life changed dramatically. It was there that I met Sharon Morgan, courted her, learned from her, fell totally in love with her, and married her. We have now shared life for more than fifty years. Along the way we added two sons, two daughters-in-law, and seven grandchildren to our family. And, through the eyes of their grandparents and in the words of Garrison Keillor, they are "all above average."

This is all the reason I need to say that enrolling as a student in 1957 at that tiny, provincial, understaffed, poorly funded school with all of its warts and flaws and shortcomings was the right move for me. In her book titled *Traveling Mercies*, Anne Lamott wrote, "I do not understand the mystery of grace—only that it meets us where we are but does not leave us where it found us."

I am forever grateful. When I was casting about, trying to find my way through a plethora of choices, at every level of life I was confronted by grace. I cannot say this is true for others, but it is my own experience. Grace met me where I was and I cling to the hope that it will finally and mysteriously lead me home. This is my faith.

7

LEAVING HOME

I was in my early teens when I first felt compelled to become a minister in the church. It was the most traumatic experience I ever had to deal with. I was broadsided by the thought. It was an idea I opposed vehemently. It was a calling, a summons to take up a vocation that I disliked, even though it was one of the things I had feared might become of me. Had I been left to my own devices, I would never have followed such a path for my life. And even though, at the time, I would have been hard-pressed to tell you what my first choice might be, becoming a clergyman most definitely would not have made even the short list.

But strangely, and in the midst of my early adolescent confusion, I felt that this was to be my divinely appointed career. Now I know that such a claim sounds audacious. It is presumptuous for anyone to think that they have been selected for some special responsibility, not by a personnel committee or through parental persuasion or peer pressure, but by God himself. Many people would say that it's delusional, and in some cases it is. Misguided people have done all sorts of unsavory things in the name of God. In fact, a comprehensive history of the world could be written around the theme of terrible things done in the name of religion. And tragically, the last such chapter is not yet written.

But there I was. Don't ask me to explain this unusual calling that ominously settled on me at a time when I was too young, too confused, and too ill-informed to make any life-altering decisions. I can't explain it; it just happened that way. Many times, however, I have thought that this personal event, coupled with my state of mind and emotions at the time, would have provided great fodder for someone's doctoral dissertation in the field of psychology.

As much as I hated the idea of being a minister, there was one other vocation that I was sure would be worse. That other thing was to feel the same sort of inner cosmic compunction to serve the church as a so-called foreign missionary. In those days the evangelical wing of the church spoke of *foreign* missions. Today, we speak of *world* missions, a less ostentatious term. In my mind it seemed that the absolutely worst thing that could happen to me, or any other unsuspecting victim, would be an overwhelming sense of being handpicked to follow such a life. I can still remember stewing over that one, worrying that I would be among those selected to spend life in far-off places dealing with primitive people and alien conditions for little or no compensation—a demanding career to be pursued over endless years of a joyless existence.

Missionaries made regular visits to our church in those early years of my life. The ubiquitous slide pictures they carried with them, providing evidence of their work, seemed to be an essential part of their anatomy. Whenever you observed a stranger packing a slide projector and screen into the church, along with a five-pound Bible, you could be pretty sure you were watching a missionary. Some of those slide shows should have been rated R. They depicted native people from undeveloped parts of the world suffering from hopeless poverty and wretched disease, including leprosy. They revealed human disaster abject enough to induce nightmares, especially in impressionable young people. All of that reinforced my conviction that this definitely was not the life for me.

Later in life I learned that I was wrong in my appraisal of those missionaries. I came to understand that the experience of living in and adapting to different cultures, something required of missionaries if they are to be effective in their work, makes for some uncommonly interesting and well-rounded individuals. I can also say that I have nothing but admiration for individuals who sacrifice their own comfort and security for others, people who minister to basic human needs not counting the cost, and who carry with them the good news of a loving God. But in my youthful judgment I did not know this; the whole business was anathema to me. And I considered my own call as the second-worst fate imaginable. It was not a happy time for me as a reluctant victim of my lot in life.

I still visualize myself on that bleak day. I was seated in the congregation of the Langley Evangelical Free Church in British Columbia's Fraser Valley, thirty miles east of Vancouver. It was a cloudy Sunday afternoon as the church gave its blessing to a large group of youth and young adults who were leaving home to spend a year or more at one of the many Bible colleges that were scattered across the Canadian prairies. In those days it was common for young adults of that place to take a year or more out of their lives to give undivided attention to the subject of being authentically Christian in whatever career, profession, or job they might pursue in the years to follow. We took our faith that seriously, while fundamentalist Bible colleges provided us the opportunity to look more closely at what such commitment might look like in the years to follow. An unstated part of the deal was that a person might be fortunate enough to find a lifelong partner along the way. Many did, and while the schools did not tout this in their official publications, you can be sure that the prospect of finding the man or the woman of one's dreams was an important consideration for many of those who went off to Bible school. Not every gesture toward spiritual purity is as pristine and innocent as it appears on the surface.

There was one particular school in a small town called Three Hills in the western province of Alberta that carried the auspicious name of Prairie Bible Institute. In some ways PBI was like an Amish community, employing students on its farm, in its workshops, and in overall care of the large campus. There was a strictly enforced rule that male and female students have nothing to do with each other. In those days they were not even allowed to talk with the opposite sex. On Sundays, when the students were encouraged to get outside and go for a walk, the men went east and the women went west. The thought being that "East is East, and West is West, and never the twain shall meet."

But they did meet. This forced segregation didn't work. It was an impossible expectation, and the telling truth is that the young men and women still found each other. So it was inevitable that when the school year came to its end there were weddings to be planned and marriages to bc solemnized. In spite of the Bible school's good but misguided intentions, the students were only doing what comes naturally.

Now on that fateful Sunday afternoon when our church gathered to give its blessing to the large group heading off to Bible college, I was slouching in the pew in a futile attempt to hide from the Almighty. I was thirteen or fourteen years old as one after another, these soon-to-be scripture scholars stood before the people in the pews and shared their stories. What was it that had led them to this point and what were their aspirations as they contemplated Bible school? Friends and relatives burst with pride as these neophyte Christians staked their claim to a higher calling. It was a heroic moment for the church. These young people were products of that church. Before them sat their families and friends, pastors and Sunday school teachers and youth counselors.

I cannot remember the substance of any one of the speeches that day. All I can say is that in the midst of this charged atmosphere, I felt a most unwelcome awareness that God was putting the finger on me. I was devastated.

It seemed that a dark shadow had fallen over my young life and that this shadow would cast its pall across all the days and years to follow. In that instant my future had been co-opted. And it was clear to me that there was nothing I could do to change things. I was trapped; there was no exit. Recalling that moment, I can truthfully say that I felt as though I were attending my own funeral before my life had even started; I had barely begun my teen years and I would carry this burden through my upcoming high school years. It was merely another form of the "Christmas Bible" in which I could find no joy.

Following my graduation from high school a friend and classmate came by my house with the sole purpose of talking me out of this crazy plan to be a minister. He spent a considerable amount of time with me that evening and I think he used good logic to marshal all the reasons why I should reconsider plans for my future. I suppose he was right. But this was not something that lent itself to logic. How do you make sense of the absurd idea that you have been chosen by divine fiat to become a clergyman, a servant, a minister of the church? My friend Eldon went away frustrated and unfulfilled later that night. And now, all these years later, I am moved that he thought highly enough of me to try to dissuade me from making such a huge mistake with my plans for the future. Sadly, Eldon died when he was only thirty years old. But how I wish I could talk with him about that conversation and about all the other things friends share after years of not seeing each other.

One of the factors that helped create my aversion to being a cleric of the church was that I did not care for clergymen. "The Reverend Mr. Grim" would have been a good moniker for those I knew personally. None of them impressed me at that early stage of my life. None of them seemed genuinely happy with their lives, most of them took themselves far too seriously, and they all made me uncomfortable when I was in their presence. To be a minister seemed like checking out of this life, turning my back on so many of the things I enjoyed, learning to talk in a way that forced God into every snippet of conversation, and waiting for the sweet hereafter when all would be bliss. What that meant, I could not say, but it didn't seem very appealing and I wanted no part of it. I have no good memories of that moment. None.

What I desperately needed was a minister as a role model; someone who seemed fulfilled in life, one who could love and serve people without losing his identity. I needed a minister who was a real person, one who was passionate about the world and its potential, one who got up in the morning and said, "This is the day the Lord has made. Let us rejoice and be glad." I know now that I yearned for one who got my attention, challenged my potential, and commanded my interest, a minister who made me seriously consider the idea that this could be a stimulating and rewarding adventure rather than a stifling withdrawal to the sidelines of life. Thinking back on that time, I believe that I wanted a spiritual leader who did not need to know it all, one who was not skittish about his own doubts and questions, perhaps a mentor who was comfortable with Herman Melville's description of the divine as somehow at one and the same time, knowable and indefinite. I wanted someone who was not out to destroy every vestige of mystery in my world.

Well, just about the time I was finishing high school, I got the man I needed. His name was David Enarson. Even apart from his vocation as a minister, he was a most winsome human being. With his wife and family of rambunctious sons he arrived as pastor of our little church and immediately breathed fresh air into our stuffy congregation, pulling back the shrouds and helping us to revel in the light. He was interesting and engaging; he was charming in the best sense of the word, and he made others want to follow his teaching for the simple reason that it had done him so much good. I remember that he would employ the word "sweetness" when he talked about his faith. All those good parts of life, things that enhanced our lives and made us better persons came under the category of that which was *sweet*. A breathtaking view of the mountains, the birth of a child, the quietude of a trout stream, an unsolicited act of human kindness, a high school graduation, a memorable sunset, a good meal shared with friends, an epiphany—all of these things were sweets from God. A sweet thing was like a blessing; in fact, in his mind, they were probably the same thing. Blessings were the sweets of life. Of course, he preached from the Bible and secured his conclusions with good stories well told. He has been my pastor emeritus for all the days of my life and I bless his memory. In fact, my last memory of David Enarson is that of his strong presence when he conducted the funeral service for my father in the winter of 1989.

A few weeks before my own retirement in 2006, the youth group from David Enarson's church of the mid-1950s, of which I was an unofficial member, and where I first struggled to come to terms with my call, gathered for a fiftieth reunion in the small town called Langley. Although we came from various places in North America, most of us once called Langley our home. Now, a half century later, we reunited at our old church, no longer at the old site, but moved to a new location. David, of course, was not there; he had already gone to that place Jesus promised to his people, the house "with many rooms"—a place of sweetness. But two of David's sons were there, now in their sixties, overweight, worn down, but carrying that same lust for life that I had seen so long ago in their father. I was asked to be the speaker at the banquet, and, among other comments, I included a heartfelt word of thanks to our very special pastor, the man who directed our feet in pleasant paths when we were all young and handsome and pretty and ready to take on the world.

It did not escape me that during those long years I had come full circle. As a young man it was here that I had first felt the terrifying call to be a minister. Well, I was back to where it all began, I was sixty-six years old, and I was anticipating my imminent retirement. That call that had come in my youth, the one I could not resist in spite of my negative feelings, had been pursued. And I felt good—fulfilled, gratified. Things that seem awful in initial perceptions are often transformed when viewed from the perspective of time.

As I reflect on my life I marvel at some of those whose paths intersected with my own. As a lost soul stumbling my way through the early teens it was John Wilson, a common name for an exceptional person who also became a clergyman. John was a five-star talent—artist, athlete, student, and much more. Virtually anything he set his mind to he could do, and do it well. And he was my friend, closer than a brother during my last two years of high school and beyond. I can't imagine how I would have fared without him. Unfortunately, we drifted apart not too many years after college and sadly John died of cancer when he was much too young.

There are so many others. These special individuals, taken together, form a great net of support and encouragement without which my life would have been diminished beyond recognition. Was it merely my good fortune to have so many angels along the way, or was something else at work, an orchestrated campaign to help me fulfill the mandate that shook me to the core when I was so very young?

But years before most of these other special people came into my life I had to make another of the great transitions of life—leaving home to pursue my vocation. It was the late summer of 1957 near the autumn equinox. Vancouver, home of the 1954 British Empire and Commonwealth Games and future host of the 2010 Winter Olympic Games, was reluctantly yielding to the changing colors and the cooling weather. Soon the landscape would be cloaked in rain, snow, more rain, and thick fog, an endless cycle that defined the fall and winter seasons in the Pacific Northwest. Such weather, coupled with the diminishing hours of daylight, was depressing to many of the residents of that soggy world; it was a constant challenge. Nowadays they have a special name for the condition: they call it seasonal affective disorder, also known as SAD.

But that year, toward the close of the 1950s and the beginning of space exploration, I was having no part of the seasonal gloom. The day had finally arrived for me to board the Canadian Pacific Railway passenger car that would take me east through the rich farmland of the Fraser River Valley to the Interior Plateau of British Columbia and on through a series of spectacular mountain ranges. Before reaching the easternmost part of my journey the train would carry me across the Cariboo, Columbia, and Selkirk Mountains and would finally wind its path over the Canadian Rockies to the edge of the vast Canadian prairies. There I would catch a commuter train called the Day Liner and speed north at a hundred miles an hour from the burgeoning city of Calgary to the twelve thousand–residents town of Red Deer in the province of Alberta. I was on my way to the small church-related college there and I was filled with excitement.

It had been quite a day, a red-letter day. Last-minute packing of my blue metal trunk that was mostly filled with clothes, good-byes to loved ones, promises to write letters home; all the usual things associated with a young man's leave-taking were part of that day. It was nearly a lifetime ago and yet I recall it vividly.

Two things stand out in my memory of that day. One was my father's reaction to what was happening to his family. He and I were standing in our small dining room, he on one side of the table and I on the other. I am not sure, but I've always thought that he might have been attempting to deliver some last words of love and advice to his second son, maybe a little speech that he had rehearsed especially for this critical moment. Everything seemed normal for the occasion and then, suddenly, his face contorted strangely and without explanation he fled down the hallway to his bedroom. It was the first and only time I saw my father cry, and it took me completely by surprise.

Years later the two of us revisited that moment and he told me what he was thinking at that special juncture in our family's life. He said he knew that this parting would change everything forever. Father knew that four years of college would have a profound effect on me and I would never come home again, not in the same way I had so many times over those first eighteen years of my life. Of course, he was right. And the time came when I too wept as I watched my own eighteen-year-old son board an airplane for Germany. The same, when my younger son left home to begin his academic career in Santa Barbara, California.

The second memorable event of that day took place at the Vancouver home of my grandparents, William and Blanche Hoffman. As they lived in the city, it made sense for us to stop there on the way to the train station. Grandpa and Grandma Hoffman, the homesteaders of southern Saskatchewan, were devout Christians, and they would not let me go without what they would have referred to as "a season of prayer."

I was not surprised by this. When I was a child I would stay with them for a few days in the summer. I remember Grandpa reading from the Bible each evening after supper and then, as we knelt at the dining room chairs, how he prayed long and loud for the protection of his large family and for the ills of the world in which they lived. So it was only natural that he would want to do the same before his grandson Charlie took his leave and blithely headed a thousand miles east for college.

It was time to pray. We knelt at the same chairs as my grandfather petitioned for my welfare: "Keep him safe, physically and spiritually. Deliver him from temptation. May he never forget the price that was paid for his salvation. Let his commitment to the will of God be constant and complete." And so, on and on, the prayer intoned the gravity of this day of departure. One would have thought that I was Joseph Conrad's Marlow setting off for the nineteenth-century African Congo and the very heart of darkness.

Meanwhile, I knelt there looking through the vertical slats of the chair back, anxious for my family, more anxious to hear Grandpa finally say "Amen," and most anxious for the moment my train would at last leave the station for the next chapter of my life. I was excited, impatient, full of hope, and more than ready to leave. It was my first great adventure on my own, and it did not disappoint.

Where it all began—road apples, dirt, a vintage car, and an endless horizon. Who could ask for anything more?

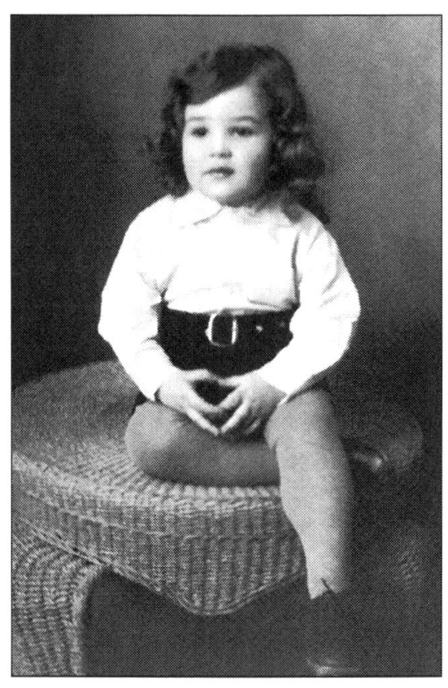

My first school, which
is now a heritage site
near Vancouver,
British Columbia

The chicken house where services were held after the Second World War.

Our 1949 house, which has since been demolished and replaced with condominiums.

My father, Willard F. Hoffman (circa 1931)

My father and mother with her dad, Benjamin Carey (circa 1932)

My paternal grandfather,
William Cyrus Hoffman,
the homesteader

My paternal grandmother,
Emily Blanche Hoffman
(née Snook), at age 49

Sharon with her parents, Helen Jesse Morgan (née Moore) and
Edwin Trevor Morgan

My parents built this cabin on the Fraser River ten miles north of Quesnel, British Columbia, with lodgepole pine and logs chinked with forest moss.

My young father, seated on ice jam front right, said his winter in the log cabin was the longest of his life.

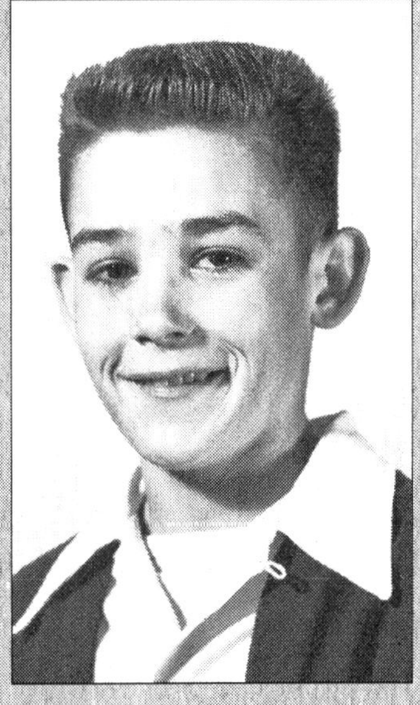

My maternal grandmother, Elizabeth Joerine, formerly Elizabeth Carey (née Luker), and my stepgrandfather, Donald Joerine ("You can't be too honest, Villard").

Me, circa 1954, about the time of my calling—the reluctant cleric.

My sister, Lorraine, aka "Bunnie," and I standing by a 1958 Ford with my high school buddy, John Wilson.

Track and field was my favorite sport in college, although I was quite mediocre.

The bus driver

A happy moment with my sister, Bunnie, and brother, Del.

Our first son,
Michael Charles 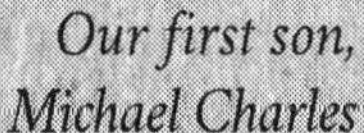

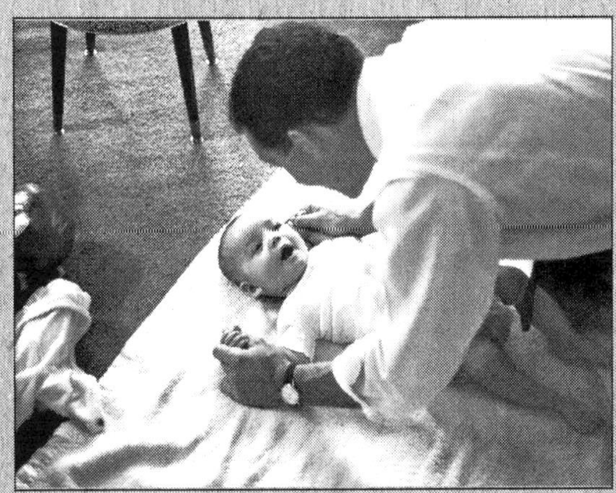

Sharon and I
with my parents
(circa 1986)

Great friends and fellow hikers: George Davis (center) and Lothair Green (right) on Canada's West Coast Trail.

David Enarson, my emeritus pastor

Emanuel Solomon Mattie, the prototype layman—we called him "Sol."

One of my 28 ascents of Half Dome

*Our second son,
Andrew Craig,
with me at the
granite monument
in the Lykens Valley,
Pennsylvania—
"Here lie
the remains of
John Peter Hoffman."*

December 29, 1960

Michael

Andrew

Our family

8

My College Days

And so it was that, in the autumn of 1957, the time of the unsettling Russian Sputnik and the equally disturbing epidemic of the Asian flu, I left home to begin my college education in Red Deer, Alberta. I was following in the footsteps of my uncle by enrolling at this Canadian educational institution, a church-related school operated by the Church of the Nazarene.

By now I am sure you are under the impression that to this point I had been shielded from the mainstream of life in North America. That impression is accurate. Now, as I headed off to college, I had no idea that the school of my choice would do little to lift the veil; its goal, although it was nowhere stated, was to confirm me in its sectarian world. But even at that, it was a broader realm than the one from which I had come and was probably a good first step in my long journey toward a measure of intellectual enlightenment and cultural awareness.

At that period of my life I was not primarily concerned about enlightenment of any sort. I was about to turn eighteen years old and I had other things on my mind. I loved sports, clothes, singing, humor, practical jokes, and good friends. Of course, I was a member of the male species so I naturally longed for a healthy relationship with an individual of the opposite sex.

I was also naive as to what constituted a liberal arts education. I suppose that in many ways I was still the blank tablet, waiting for my story to be written. I was a college freshman who had only the vaguest ideas of what he was supposed to accomplish with a college career. I innocently thought that course grades were the important things, and as long as a student achieved passing grades everything would be fine. So, I learned how to pass tests but too often I left the real learning behind.

Eventually some of my official and unofficial teachers began to get through to me about what was entailed on the path to authentic education. But, in college, it was not until my senior year that I began seriously to apply myself, and by then I had developed unproductive learning habits that blocked my path to becoming *a bona fide* student. I learned the hard lesson that patterns grooved over many years are not easily changed.

Perhaps I should elaborate a little on my earlier life as a student. I never had the opportunity to attend kindergarten. For me, life as a student began in the first grade. I was five years old at the time, but would turn six a few weeks after school started in that fall of 1945. I performed well that year and the next—first and second grades. During the third grade I missed a lot of school because of various childhood illnesses and I fell behind. To make matters worse, we moved during that school year and I found myself in an unknown setting struggling to catch up with the class. Somehow, I made it and was promoted to the fourth grade. Now I felt as though I was on the same page as the rest of my class. Also, I had something to prove to myself having to do with my own abilities as a student. I worked hard, got my teacher's attention, and averaged above ninety percent with my grades. Then, once again, we moved, and for me it meant another school for the start of my fifth grade. It was not long until this new teacher felt that I should be promoted to the next grade and that I was more than ready for the next level of work. What this meant is that I took two grades in one year—fifth and sixth. Not only that, I also moved to another new school for the sixth grade.

It was at this time that I started to coast with my studies, and was content merely to get by. I told myself that I could outperform my fellow students if I wanted to, and I believed it. So began a downward spiraling of my academic life that continued for years. I was not only the youngest child in the class, I was also the smallest. But I craved attention so I became the class clown, the court jester. Give me the floor and I will get people laughing. That is how I made my way over the years ahead, including both high school and college.

My college was painfully small. And while this had many disadvantages, it also presented opportunities that would have been unavailable in a larger setting. For example, I had some wonderful experiences with music—college choir and men's vocal quartet in particular. On occasion I even sang solos. The truth is that I simply loved to sing, had a tolerable voice, could carry a tune on pitch, and was capable of learning a harmony line. So it was that, with my limited talents and the indulgence of three other men, I was privileged to sing in a number of male quartets and mixed voice choirs. We offered our music in college chapel services, in outlying churches, at special events—wherever we were invited. On two occasions I was part of a group that toured our educational jurisdiction during the spring and summer when college classes were in recess.

For me, the tour of 1960 stands out; it was the summer before my senior year of college. We traveled fourteen thousand miles by car, performing in scores of churches on weekday evenings, in Sunday worship services, and at the occasional special event. The purpose of our endeavor was to raise financial support for our school, to spread goodwill, and to recruit students. I cannot say how well we succeeded in that goal, but I can say that it was a once-in-a-lifetime adventure. Although we received modest remuneration for our services, none of us became wealthy. There was not the remotest possibility that we would be mistaken for the Beatles and rewarded accordingly. But we did not complain; it was truly an unforgettable opportunity. I should, however, tell you that one member of that quartet went on to earn his doctorate in music, one was already teaching music at our own school, and another, who sang with us the previous year also completed a doctorate in music and taught in one of Canada's universities. Our baritone, after earning his doctorate, went on to teach at the seminary and to serve the church as a missionary in Haiti, Brazil, and other places. The water in which I sailed was rich with talent.

Although we did not make it as far east as Newfoundland, we literally covered the continental part of Canada from coast to coast, from Vancouver Island in the west to Prince Edward Island in the east. And, as this was the year of the Church of the Nazarene quadrennial assembly in Kansas City, Missouri, we sang there as well. Most of the time our energies were spent performing in rural churches in small towns with names such as Moose Jaw, Medicine Hat, Swift Current, Picture Butte, Dawson Creek, Langley, and Sundre. But we also sang in Chicago, Detroit, Montreal, Toronto, Vancouver, Edmonton, Calgary, and Winnipeg. On a layover in Boston we listened as the Boston Pops gave a concert on the green. And we visited the famed Fenway Park to watch the Boston Red Sox play baseball. In Prince Edward Island we feasted on lobster, for most of us a new experience. There, too, a kindly fisherman offered to take us fishing early one morning. When we showed up at dawn on a dark and windy day and saw the heavy seas, I knew this would not be my day. So I was greatly relieved when the fisherman came to the door of his shack, looked at his familiar corner of the Atlantic, shook his head, and said, "Not today."

Two of us in that vagabond quartet were engaged to be married, and I was one of the two. As this was long before the advent of e-mail and cell phones, I lived for those days when a letter would catch up to me from my fiancée. And that is another chapter of my college experience I want to share.

I saw her for the first time in the fall of 1957. She was majoring in music, specializing in piano performance, and her name was Sharon Morgan. Early in my first year, as I joined the male pastime of discussing college women, I heard about her. To say that those men in the dormitory talked about her in hushed tones would be an overstatement. Nevertheless, there were few of us who would not have welcomed the chance to date her. She was at the top of the who's who list. But she was dating Superman, off limits to us peons—look but don't touch. We all accepted that. Sharon and her beau moved in another universe, so we had to look elsewhere. If I was a little ambivalent as to whether I might one day have the chance to date Sharon Morgan, my roommate, Don, would reel me in with generous doses of reality as he saw it. He was emphatic: "Stay away from her, Chuck. You'll only get hurt."

But I was seeing another reality that supported some of my wishful thinking, a potentially dangerous development. At various times I was aware that this same Miss Morgan was looking my way and smiling. So, to paraphrase an old country and western song, "I was looking back to see if she was looking back to see if I was looking back to see if she was looking back at me." It's an old game. And sure enough, it was not long until she gave Superman his flight instructions and she and I became an item. "OK, roommate Don, what do you think of that?"

I think we had a few good times, but I'm not sure. She knew she was not ready for a serious relationship. The same thing was true for me, but I did not know it. So it was impossible for her to make me understand why she was sending me off to join Superman in his hopeless flights through the inscrutable atmosphere of womanhood. Now, not only was I naive, I was also bitter, depressed, confused, and hurt. What floored me was that, in spite of our breakup, we were to remain good friends, and I had no idea how such a thing could be possible.

I saw her on campus every day, watched her relating with others, and eventually saw her forming a romantic relationship with a friend of mine. He was the best-looking guy at the college, a Hollywood-handsome Robert Redford who was both an athlete and a budding musician. It took the wind out of my sails and left the sails lying at my feet.

In a manifestly politically incorrect statement Oscar Wilde once said that "Crying is for plain women. Pretty women go shopping." I suppose there's some truth somewhere in that sentiment, but I would not state it as universal. What I do know is that when Sharon Morgan ended our relationship I went shopping. In fact, I did not give up. I still had a little money in my bank account so I did what men such as I have done in one way or another for generations. I went out and bought some new clothes in order to enhance my own looks and impress her. That didn't work, so I did the opposite. I got myself a haircut that I knew she would *not* like—anything to get her attention. In those days I still had hair, a whole head of hair, and I combed it in an Elvis Presley style. But on this occasion I got what they call a buzz. I might as well have saved the effort because nothing worked. And I could hear the echo of Don's earlier words of advice: "Stay away from her, Chuck. You'll only get hurt."

The following school year I spent a lot of effort to convince myself that my grand romance with Sharon Morgan was truly over. And I dated someone else, a friend to this day and a soul mate during those college years. Meanwhile, Sharon continued to be wooed by her talented Mr. Redford as we passed through the abbreviated autumn of 1958 and the long winter of 1959. I think I was doing my best, but I still couldn't get over her. First loves have amazing staying power and the wound prevailed. Don was right.

Spring finally arrived. By then I was driving a school bus, partly in order to maintain my penchant for nice clothes and partly to pay my college expenses. The routine was to pick up airmen and deliver them to the air base a few miles south of Red Deer. Then, on my way back to town, I would collect high school students from the outlying farms and deliver them to the composite high school in town. One morning, after an unusually heavy rainfall the night before, and after I had made my way to the air base but before my first stop for students, I had an accident. The country road on which I traveled that morning was treacherous. It had the consistency of grease, which the locals appropriately named gumbo. It was impossible to drive that road without the rear of the bus fishtailing back and forth. This was especially true when the vehicle was empty. The trick, according to a professional driver with whom I had consulted, was to maintain just the right speed, not too slow and not too fast.

I will never know on which side of that continuum I erred, but unwittingly I allowed the back right dual wheels to leave the road surface. When that happened it was just a matter of time before those same rear wheels pulled the vehicle off the roadway. Prairie roads were built up until they traversed the plains well above the fields; it was actually a long way down from the road level to the field level. I still remember the violence of the crash as the big bus fell on its side, glass breaking, seats flying, metal bending, and I, *sans* seat belt, being tossed out of my driver's seat and into the stairwell.

Thankfully, I was not hurt. I escaped coming to that violent rest without the vehicle on top of me. But, more importantly, I was the only person on the bus when it dropped off the road. I remember thinking of prairie gophers crawling out of their burrows as I emerged from the driver's side window to face the nightmare I had just created. The long and short of it was that the bus company rehired me for the next year. They said that they were impressed with my driving, even if I had to turn the bus over to get their attention.

That was fine, but the one whose attention I really wanted was Sharon Morgan. And as the spring of 1959 inched its way over our world with new life I sensed that there might be new life for me as well. There was nothing dramatic at first, just little things, small gestures that made my heart skip a beat. Then it was time for our college choir to make its annual spring tour. This time the itinerary would take us west to Vancouver and then across the Strait of Georgia to Vancouver Island and the provincial capital of Victoria. We were on the return crossing back to the mainland and, as they say, "It was a dark and stormy night." The seas were heavy and some of the larger vehicles, including our tour bus that I was *not* driving, were specially anchored to the ship's lower deck for fear they would be shifted as the ship rode out the storm.

Do not ask me how we knew, but both Sharon and I were aware that we were about to end our current romantic relationships and be free to explore other options. And, as it turns out, she was as aware of me as I was of her. We were both on the brink of committing serious romance.

Here's what happened on the ferry crossing that night. I had purchased some snack food and then ventured onto the ship's deck outside the spacious passenger cabin. I remember how the seawater sprayed as the storm winds blew. I have always imagined human warmth and affection being intensified under such circumstances; even as a small child tucked under my covers and hearing the gale howling its way through the forest, it seemed the best place to experience at one and the same time the storm without and the serenity within. So there I was with my bag of snacks, alone, when out of nowhere she appeared. It was a little like Jesus appearing to the disciples on the road to Emmaus as they attempted to come to terms with their loss. Suddenly it was the two of us alone on the exposed deck. I have no idea what we said to each other but it was probably something about the storm. It didn't matter; we could have said anything or nothing. I do recall that I offered her some of whatever it was that I was snacking on. We did not linger—only a few minutes—or was it less than a minute? By then the deed was done and neither of us has ever forgotten it. Volumes could be written on what we did not say but still communicated to each other at that unforgettable moment. There was eloquence in our silence that only lovers understand.

We were actually standing on the narrow, slippery, port side of a ferryboat bobbing its way through a nasty sea with a bitterly cold wind biting through our clothing. But we might as well have been together at midnight in the tropics with a full moon, shimmering stars, fleecy clouds, and a soft breeze as our cruise liner silently sailed its way through the pliant sea. Beauty and romance are definitely in the eye of the beholder; also in the heart.

In just a few short weeks we had our first date. We had dinner together at Red Deer's Peacock Inn, not knowing that in less than two years and with our guests we would sit down for our wedding reception at the same establishment. But following dinner that evening of what was really a new first date we drove to a resort area called Sylvan Lake. There we sat and talked about all that had happened to us during the past eighteen months. I felt like an alien finally coming home. We listened to the car radio, especially to the song, "What a Difference a Day Makes." Everything felt right; my world was back on its axis.

The wedding took place in the college chapel on Thursday, December 29, 1960. Sharon's sister Carole was matron of honor, my brother Del was best man, my sister Lorraine was a bridesmaid, and my wonderful friend and erstwhile advisor, Don, was there, too, as one of my groomsmen. Alas, his predictions as to what would happen to me if I set my heart on Sharon Morgan were finally proved groundless. And I know that even he was happy for me. Especially is this true when I tell you that Beth, the woman Don would later marry, was also one of our bridesmaids.

So that was how things came to pass for me during the days and years of my college education.

9

I REMEMBER

I don't think I am what is called an Anglophile, but I do have a soft spot for things British. More to the point, I am partial to my own romanticized idea of British life. Growing up in what was then called the Dominion of Canada, a strong member of the British Commonwealth of Nations, left a permanent mark on my life. I was part of the world where schoolchildren still sang "God Save the King" under the reign of George VI and "God Save the Queen" under the reign of his daughter, Queen Elizabeth II. I may not have felt so partial to the English if I lived in parts of the empire where the class system was still in place. I never had to face this in Canada.

Another British influence on my life is the fact that my maternal grandmother immigrated from England to Canada in 1912. Her maiden name was Elizabeth Luker and at the time she lived in London. She was eighteen years old and that year, the date of the *Titanic* tragedy at sea—the sinking of a ship that was thought to be unsinkable. Grandmother claimed that she had initially booked passage on the maiden voyage of that great passenger liner but fortunately for her and many others, including myself, she had to change her travel plans at the last minute.

And then there was an autumn day in 1951. That was the year the young Princess Elizabeth of England visited British Columbia; a sunny day in October when I stood with others for hours by the Trans Canada Highway waiting to see her motorcade pass by. Soon after that her father, King George VI, died and the young princess became Queen Elizabeth II. Her reign has lasted more than sixty years, a term longer even than that of Queen Victoria. I know that it is all pomp and circumstance, too costly a luxury, controversial even in the British Isles, and confusing to the rest of the world. But I would not want to see the institution abandoned as long as there are people such as Elizabeth sitting on the throne and comprehending its historical, if symbolical, significance.

As I write this I can almost hear some of my British friends saying, "Hoffman, you don't know what you're talking about. You have never lived in Great Britain. You have no firsthand experience with the subject. You are turning a blind eye to all the things wrong with British imperialism and British empire building, along with the British class system. You have never had people look down the length of their long noses at you simply because you don't know how to make a good cup of tea. You have never been shifted into a predetermined slot simply because of an accent shaped in your earlier years." And all I can do is agree; I am guilty on all counts. But I still nurture my quixotic feelings about a British world that to a great degree no longer exists. I suppose it is common to idealize parts of life because the realities are often hard to face.

A British television production that has captivated the imagination of much of the world's watchers is the upscale soap opera called *Downton Abbey*. It is a long-running saga of the British upper class and its army of servants, all of who inhabit one of the great estates in the Yorkshire countryside. The chronicle begins in 1912. Word has just arrived that the *Titanic* has crashed into an iceberg and sank into the frigid depths of the North Atlantic. Along with hundreds of others, the heir to the Downton fortune has died in this marine disaster.

This death changes everything for these upper class people and their servants, and launches a family narrative that millions of people worldwide have followed as a television drama. Even in the twenty-first century the loss of the *Titanic* remains a significant date in our memory—an epic event in world history. And there are many other famous and infamous milestones: the Battle of Hastings in 1066 on the southeast coast of England, the Battle of the Plains of Abraham in 1759 at Quebec City, the plague that swept Europe in the fourteenth century, the worldwide influenza pandemic of 1918 and 1919 that killed more people than had died in the Great War. And, of course, there is the horrendous attack on America, fresh in our memories, which we now refer to simply as 9/11. These and many other happenings frame our lives and influence how we live them.

That said, I want to share some of the events that I personally recall as I reminisce about my own "three score and ten years." Looking back in time, I separate myself from the present and see myself as a small boy, as a youth, a young adult, a middle-aged man, and now as one who is a senior citizen. It all went by so fast.

In one of my earliest memories I see myself walking down an unpaved country road on my way home from visiting with friends. I am newly aware that the president of the United States, Franklin D. Roosevelt, has just died. It is early April 1945 and his death moves me even though I am only five years old. Reflecting on that sad day I recall how children of that time and place, even in Canada, had a natural affinity for whomever it was that occupied the presidency of the United States of America. In our youthful innocence we were not aware of politics. In our unsophisticated understanding we reasoned that America was a great nation so it followed that America's leader, no matter who it was, must be great as well. That's what we thought, and in our minds he always was. Roosevelt, along with Gene Autry and Roy Rogers of the movie Westerns, were three of my heroes when I was very young. Many years later I know that life is more complex than it seemed at the time. It is one of the reasons why I've told others that I am not as sure about things as I used to be; I knew more then than I know now. And I am aware that every leader of any consequence runs the risk of ending up with a sketchy record of accomplishments. Roosevelt was no exception, but to me as a small boy he was simply too important to die.

The death of that US president near the end of the Second World War is one of the things I will always remember.

I recall a time a few weeks later that same year of 1945. I was with my paternal grandmother and we were riding a streetcar in downtown Vancouver. It was late August. News had just reached the public about Japan's unconditional surrender to the Allied forces. After years of brutal warfare, including the nuclear bombings of two Japanese cities and the horrendous loss of life, the Pacific campaign had finally ended. Inasmuch as Hitler's Germany and Mussolini's Italy had already fallen to the Allies, we were not surprised when Imperial Japan collapsed as well. But it had taken longer than we expected, and it took President Harry Truman's controversial decision to drop the bombs before it actually happened. One of the things that stands out for me is the general state of excitement and euphoria that swept over the growing crowds of people in the streets of Vancouver that day. I am sure it was this way all over North America and other parts of the world, too, as war-weary citizens embraced each other and celebrated the news we had waited so long to greet.

The other thing that remains in my memory of that day is my grandmother's sense of urgency in getting home before those streets became clogged with merrymakers. There was nothing in her Pennsylvania Dutch heritage that could allow spontaneity to supersede practicality. So it was homeward and away from the fray for the two of us.

By this time I knew what it was to live life under the constant hassle of rationing goods. By 1945, Canada, as a member of the British Commonwealth, had been at war for nearly six years. For Canada, the war began the moment Great Britain declared war on Adolf Hitler in September 1939. This took place with Germany's invasion of Poland and now it was over. So I was excited to think that this system of allotments, the inevitable accompaniment to war, would finally come to an end. At last, we would have gasoline and tires for our cars, plenty of butter and meat for our tables, and an abundance of toys for our amusements. Even as a young child who had not yet entered school, I was aware of these wartime restrictions, and it was not long until I went out and spent fifty cents on a rubberized balloon, a considerable sum for a five-year-old to spend on such a toy.

One of the memories that I can't leave out concerns not a single event but things that took place over a period of less than three years at the Willoughby Elementary School a half mile from our small, ten-acre farm on what was then McLarty Road and is now 80th Avenue in Langley. This chapter of my life began two years following the move of our family from Saskatchewan to British Columbia in 1943. It marks the beginning of my formal education. I see myself sitting in the classroom of our one-room school. My teacher was Mrs. Jamison and she was directing her efforts toward us first graders. She was responsible for at least four grades in that small room. There may have been as many as six grades; I can't remember for sure. It was our very first lesson in learning how to read and, more specifically, it was about phonics. Mrs. Jamison began with the letter *a* and the letter *m*. She wanted us to know the sounds of these two letters that she had written on the blackboard. It was a first step in getting us to *sound out* a word. So she asked the question, "What does the baby say when she tastes something sweet?" The correct answer was *ah* or *mmm*, the sounds of the two letters before us. And then she pointed to the letters individually and asked us to sound out the letter. The class was quick to respond with the correct answers. At least, most of the class responded; I said nothing, thinking that the whole exercise was a bit childish. So I remained silent. After all, I was five years old, would turn six in a month, and wanted no part in these juvenile games. But it didn't seem to matter. By the end of that first year I was ranked the number-one student in the first grade, one of the numerous times I was a big fish in a very, very small pond.

Fifty-five years later I was visiting my ailing mother where she lived just outside Vancouver. By that time my father had died, so it was just Mother and I. On a clear winter day we decided to get in the car and drive to some of the sites where much of our lives were lived long years before. We set out to find the sacred ground where our 1949 house once stood, where we raised a couple hundred chickens to augment the family income, and where I had spent the formative years of my youth. But we were disappointed. The house had been torn down and the entire area was covered with condominiums. We were not sure exactly where our house once stood, this modest bungalow that represented so much of our past. Both Mother and I experienced a deep sense of loss. That house held so many memories for us, so with bruised hearts and a deep sense of loss we got back into the car and resumed our nostalgic journey through the past.

Soon we found ourselves outside the buildings that were the Willoughby Elementary School. And there it was—the old building, my first school. It was well cared for, having gone through so many iterations over the years. We took turns photographing each other as we stood in the snow on the outside of the structure. But not only had the authorities taken good care of my old school, they were still using it. And in a moment a young teacher appeared on the stoop outside the very room where Mrs. Jamison taught me to read so many years ago. The teacher asked if he could help us. I told him of my relationship to the school and he invited Mother and me into his classroom. The room was full of children; class was in session. I looked around to see nothing but nameless faces; all of my friends were gone, but in that fleeting moment we had all returned to take our places at the wooden desks with their wrought-iron hardware, their slanted tops, their small bookshelves under the desktops, their slots for pens and pencils, and their inkwells.

At some point during my first year at that school I sang my first public solo. I stood before my classmates with my teacher looking on and I sang a popular song titled, "You Are My Sunshine." It's a love song and the singer expresses the sentiment that his girlfriend makes him happy even "when skies are gray." Gray skies pretty much described the weather of our northwestern world, so we understood the lyrics. And by this time I had a girlfriend. She was also in the first grade and her name was Judy. I wonder if I thought of her as I crooned out the song, doing my best to sound like Gene Autry, the singing cowboy who had popularized the piece. By that juncture in my life I had already listened to a lot of country and western music on the radio. It came from a program called *Bill Rae's Roundup* and it was aired over station CKNW in New Westminster. Listening to that program was a poor substitute for kindergarten but it entertained me during the time I waited impatiently to begin the first grade.

It was from that program that I also learned how to yodel, which I was occasionally asked to do by various people, including my cousin Bonnie who knew that this was a way of getting under my skin. I especially remember a neighboring German couple who asked me to display my yodeling prowess for them one morning as they were enjoying their coffee. I can still see and smell that coffee. It was strong coffee laced with fresh cream and sugar and drank from porcelain-lined tin mugs. And as if that wasn't enough pleasure for this contented couple, they wanted to be serenaded as well. I remember that I was a little self-conscious about meeting their request. I knew even that early in my life, that I enjoyed being the center of attention as long as I had complete control of things. But my German friends wore me down until I struck a compromise and decided to take the risk. I ended up yodeling from behind a tree in their backyard where they could hear but not see me.

I have no idea as to whether my performance was a success. I do know that my girlfriend Judy never asked me to yodel, and neither did any of my other grade one classmates. But it doesn't matter. Who ever heard of a yodeling solo without accompaniment? I did learn some time later that yodeling in Europe is different than what you get from

American cowboys, so the German couple was probably disappointed with my behind-the-tree concert. That was the only time they asked me to render a personal performance. However, I was serious about country and western music. A couple years later, in fact, I saved up ten dollars and bought a guitar through a mail order catalog. I might as well have kept the money because the lessons I needed were not to be had and, many years later, the guitar became history when my brother employed it to hit someone over the head with at a wild party. He had seen it done with great effect in a Western movie and by that time I had given up on the instrument anyway.

Sharon and I made another visit to my old schoolhouse in the late summer of 2014. I was apprehensive as to whether it would still be there. But as I rounded the corner heading south at the intersection of 80th Avenue and 208th Street in the township of Langley, there it was. It had been well cared for and I was elated to see that it was being preserved as a heritage site.

Now before I move on with these recollections I must tell you the names of some of the people who populated my world at this time of my early schooling. There was Mike Berschtinski and his friend Lawrence Smurthwaite, both of whom struggled with academic pursuits and fell far short of social expectations. They labored to make their way in life and, I'm sorry to say, the rest of us were more interested in being amused by them than we were with helping them. Then there was Harry Ellens. Harry was a year or two ahead of me in our one-room schoolhouse and had already been subjected to Mrs. Jamison's phonics lessons. It may be that this had left a scar on his psyche, that manifested itself in Harry's annoying habit of chewing playdough. Our teacher, whose job was to educate a whole room full of colorful characters, was determined to break Harry of his disgusting practice. On one occasion she had him sit on a chair facing the rest of the class and forced him to chew a large wad of the offending matter. I remember feeling sorry for poor Harry as he soldiered on through his tears and spittle and substitute chewing gum. I don't know for sure, but I assume he had second thoughts the next time he thought about chomping down on his playdough.

One summer day my brother and I somehow ended up at Harry's house. We were sitting in the cramped kitchen with him and his mother. A twirl of flypaper hung from the ceiling with the carcasses of a few black flies permanently attached to its sweet seduction. That was stimulation enough for my brother and me but there was more to the scene; one of the four walls of the kitchen was literally black with flies. These flies had nothing holding them there; they were free to come or go or even to take off and land on the flypaper if that was their choice. Mrs. Ellens was dumbfounded by the state of her kitchen wall. She said that she could not for the life of her understand the strange behavior of these flies. After all, she pointed out to us, she had left the door open all day so they could escape. It's a little like drilling a hole in the bottom of the boat to let the water out.

A stone's throw from our house was the small shack populated by the widower Mr. McCauley and his children, including Winnie, Bernie, Michael, and their little sister.

It was a desperate situation and I know that my parents, especially my mother, had entertained the idea of trying to adopt the little girl.

In those days public health was a concern, so the schools conducted what were called health checks for the schoolchildren. This was a hardship for Winnie and Bernie. Things such as carrying a clean handkerchief, having unsoiled fingernails, washing the face, and cleaning the teeth were on the list of things to be checked. One morning Mrs. Jamison was in the midst of her list of hygienic interrogations when she asked Winnie if she had brushed her teeth that morning. "No," Winnie responded, "I couldn't brush my teeth because Bernie was using the toothbrush!" This is definitely not what the health authorities had in mind when they instituted their program of personal hygiene. Clearly, they should have been more specific with their health care instructions.

Then there was Leonard Frick. Leonard was a little older than I, went to the Willoughby school, and lived with the rest of his family on Render Road a half mile from my house. I remember being at his place one day when the family was having lunch. I sat on a chair away from their table and watched the proceedings from my front-row seat. It was quite entertaining. Circling around the table and begging for food was their little dog, a mixed breed of the canine species with a preponderance of terrier in its pedigree. I noticed the dog sitting on its haunches and looking toward the table as if to say, "What about me?" A family member closest to the animal, it could have been Leonard, took special notice of the dog, reprimanded it for begging, hit its upturned nose with his fork, licked off the fork, and resumed the task of devouring his lunch. Where is the health brigade when you need it? I couldn't wait to get home and tell my dad about that one.

Referencing these interesting characters whose paths I crossed early in my life is not meant to present our family as a shining example of what is considered the prim and the proper. We had our own problems; we were not all spit and polish ourselves. Lack of modern plumbing made much of life difficult and sometimes it was easy to skip the traditional Saturday night bath in a washtub. This was especially the case during the cold and damp winter months. We had no central heating, so bathing in a washtub in a drafty kitchen was not one of our favorite experiences. Following our baths we climbed into frigid beds at night and got up in the morning to subfreezing temperatures in the bedroom. Having grown up under these conditions may be the reason why it wasn't until I was forty years old that I considered backpacking and camping as viable forms of recreation. Much of my childhood had been like an endless backpacking trip and when the time finally came to modernize, I welcomed it with great enthusiasm.

Five short years after the end of the Second World War, conflict began on the Korean Peninsula, a war lasting from June of 1950 until July of 1953. By this time our family had moved into the house on Latimer Road, the house my father had built in 1949. Looking back to that time I see myself standing by the kitchen table on my return from Latimer Road School and reading the news about this Korean War as it appeared in the *Vancouver Sun* newspaper. I was on the verge of being a teenager and I feared the uncertain days ahead. I had enough memory of the latest war and its aftermath to know that such news could have a negative impact on my own life and it saddened me. I gave no thought to the fate of those participants on both sides of the conflict, along with their families, who would personally go through the trauma and loss of war. My apathy was a sign of my own immaturity and self-absorption.

Another significant event that I recall was the death of the USSR president and dictator Joseph Stalin. Again, the newspaper is part of the picture. It was 1953 and on this occasion I am delivering the newspaper. At one time or another I had distributed both the *Vancouver Sun* and the *Vancouver Daily Province* newspapers, riding my bicycle over country roads and leaving papers in mailboxes. It's a rainy day and I'm probably pretty wet; soaked to the skin, in fact. Most of my customers have no television, and if they have been away from the radio that day they will first learn of the tyrant's death when they open the paper and see the headline. As with the majority of my contemporaries, an age group known as the silent generation, I am weak on world affairs at that moment in time. But I am aware of the Cold War and I know that Stalin is not one of the good guys. I learned in later life that this was a gross understatement. I learned also that this leader of the Kremlin was a monster, responsible for murdering millions of innocent people during the course of his sordid life. Stalin allowed his obsession with turning the Soviet Union into a world superpower to blind him to the dictates of morality of the most basic sort. He died March 5, 1953, at the age of seventy-four. As I write these memories I am a senior citizen, older than he was at the time of his death.

An important development of the Cold War was the race into outer space between the USSR and the USA. As a freshman college student in 1957, I watched as the Soviets and their Sputnik got there first. It was a blow to American pride and confidence and it stirred the country to catch up and surpass the Russian accomplishments. I remember not being surprised by the result of this determination. Watching from my choice seat north of the Canada/US border, I felt that America could do just about anything it set out to get done. I may have been wrong to assume such a thing, but in this case I was right. The "small step for man, one giant leap for mankind" was taken twelve years later in July of 1969 as Neil Armstrong and Buzz Aldrin planted their feet on the surface of the moon. I remember Sharon taking our four-year-old son Michael outdoors and having him look at the moon. "Michael," she said, "There are men standing on the moon this evening. Look up there and always remember this moment."

So things in space went well for America, but things on Earth presented massive challenges. Did America believe in the freedom of religion or did it not? Did America deem that a Roman Catholic could become president of the United States? Did it accept as true the equality of all humans or did it hold that some parts of the population were less equal than others? Did America really believe in gender equality? Or did it judge that women should be kept in their place as men defined that place? And what about the question of war? When and under what conditions was it justified? More specifically, what were we to do with the war in Vietnam? These were hard questions for a society that had never fully questioned its long-established norms and practices; controversial questions for a country that, for much of its history, had avoided the hard task of self-examination. And there was more of this sort of thing to come in the years ahead, especially during the 1960s and 1970s. It was a time of painful national introspection.

In the midst of these challenges a number of dreadful things took place. It was October 1962. I was a second-year seminary student in Kansas City, Missouri, as I sat with others of my classmates and professors in the school's chapel. We were singing a hymn. In those days there were very few women in the seminary so as we sang we sounded like a robust male chorus. On this particular occasion we all wondered if our world was about to destroy itself. The Soviet Union and the United States of America were facing off in what was called the Cuban Missile Crisis. The boorish President Khrushchev was pushing his luck; the young President Kennedy was sailing in uncharted waters. So we were living with a great sense of uncertainty; it was a precarious moment in world history. Both sides possessed nuclear power, meaning that the stakes were even higher than any of us could imagine. Our future, as we sang together that autumn day in the seminary chapel, was a very large question mark. I will never forget the words to the hymn we sang at that poignant moment:

When peace like a river attendeth my way
When sorrows like sea billows roll
Whatever my lot Thou hast taught me to say
It is well, it is well with my soul.

Looking back now I realize that the meaning of those words clearly bends toward a self-centered outlook on life. That is, no matter what goes on in this world I, with my otherworldly orientation, am safe. Obviously, those words say nothing about the Russian or Cuban or American innocents whose lives might have been impacted by that situation. This sensitivity I would have to learn in the years to come.

Nevertheless, it remains true that there are times in life when, from the wellsprings of faith, we discern the appropriate word to the existential moment. I realize now that, for me, it is not something I can generate by my own efforts. It is something that emerges unbidden and spontaneous. That moment in a seminary chapel, at a time when the two most powerful nations in the world rattled their sabers, was one such time.

As I attended lectures, wrote papers, and prepared for examinations over three years of seminary training in Kansas City, Missouri, Sharon worked in one of the international offices of our denomination. Her workplace was a short walk from the seminary so we would often get together for lunch. It was the twenty-second of November in 1963. As we sat down for our meal together in the cafeteria we started hearing sketchy news briefs over the intercom. In a short period of time we learned that something terrible had taken place in Dallas, Texas.

The thirty-ninth president of the United States of America, John Fitzgerald Kennedy, had been shot by a sniper in that city and rushed to a hospital with grievous wounds. Soon we learned that he had died. Over the next few days we watched as America, convulsed with grief and confusion, tried to assimilate and learn from the gravity of such insanity within its own ranks. It was a hard lesson, only partially learned. The killings continued with other victims, including Martin Luther King Jr. and Robert Kennedy, the late president's brother.

All of us who were old enough recall where we were on that fateful day of 1963. I remember the event well but I also remember how ill prepared I was to process such momentous news. The sentiments I felt as a seminary student singing, "It is well with my soul," in the midst of the Cuban Missile Crisis were absent. My understanding of national and international issues was superficial and uninformed. My political instincts were strangely aligned with my hidebound traditionalist theology. This may have been acceptable for some but, in my case, there had been no serious reflection on the subject; I had embraced a point of view without asking questions or thinking about consequences. I am ashamed to admit it, but I saw the Kennedy assassination as opening the door for Richard Nixon to become president, a thought that now embarrasses me. But this is truly the sentiment that occupied my mind as I returned to the seminary on that fateful day, a feeling that I strongly suspect was held by the vast majority of those who shared with me the same ecclesiastical and theological subculture.

I am grateful for an evolution of my thinking, which more honestly reflects my thoughts and feelings in both theology and politics. Today I am far removed from those earlier held positions. If forced to label my stance today, I would say that I am a progressive conservative. I look back and respect long-held traditions while at the same time I strive to maintain an open mind to innovation. I want neither to be trapped by the past nor to be intimidated by the future, believing that the old and the new must remain in a creative tension. Out of this acknowledged stress come new forms and new ideas to serve, to resource, and to inform my present living. This is often hard work, but it is absolutely vital. It involves me in exciting enterprises of the imagination and can lead to helpful changes. It is the path to resourcefulness, the way to inventiveness and production. Such hard work requires the traditionalists and the progressives to remain in honest, informed conversation that respects the other and seeks to understand—an activity that seems in these days to have eluded both our political and our religious leaders.

In 1991 I moved from San Diego where, for ten years, I had worked under Mark Trotter, senior minister at First United Methodist Church. I had been appointed to lead a church located to the north of San Diego, so I was somewhat preoccupied with the challenges of my new assignment. However, the fall of the Soviet Union did not escape my attention. This event was something that had been part of our hopes and prayers for many years. And even though such a momentous happening solved one of the most vexing problems of our world, it created other troubles that awaited the world's consideration. Among other things, we learned that troubles among nations that had been put on hold for seventy years were now resumed to the detriment of far too many individuals and groups. The cost in human life was considerable.

Ten years later I was lying on a cot in a cabin in Yosemite National Park in the Sierra Nevada Mountains of California. As was my custom those days, I was listening to my radio in that early morning of September 11, 2001. The previous day I had hiked with others to the summit of a mountain called Half Dome. I had done it many times before but it was always a unique experience because each trek presented its own challenges, especially as I grew older. It was difficult to get clear radio signals in the park, so initially I didn't know what I had awakened to. As I pieced things together I realized that at some time during the night I had tuned my radio to a music station. But what I was hearing was not music. It was two men in that radio station discussing something they were seeing on a television monitor. They had obviously turned off the music to report on what was unfolding on the screen before them. Initially, they were not sure themselves. But a clear picture was emerging and it became evident that airplanes had flown into the twin towers of the World Trade Center in New York City. America was under attack from sinister forces and the magnitude of the siege was unfathomable. The event grew in size as other stories came to light about the attack on the Pentagon and the forced crash of an airliner in Pennsylvania. The loss of life was staggering.

With heavy hearts we left the park that morning listening to radio reports as we made our way back to our homes some four hundred miles away in Southern California. It was a sobering journey. People soon began comparing this attack with that on Pearl Harbor in 1941, and we knew that life for us would never be the same again. That evening, under the leadership of my colleague, Melanie Silva, we held a service at our church to think about, affirm, and access our faith, even and especially in such a time as this national and international tragedy. A decade and a half later the world is still trying to deal with the events of 9/11. I believe that America's reaction has too often missed the mark and been bungled, wrongheaded, and ill devised. It is tragically lacking in positive outcomes, as we have played into the hands of those who seek us ill.

Now most of the personal memories that I have shared can be pinpointed to some specific occurrence and place in time. What I have written is not intended as a history lesson. In fact, important things have been omitted from my list—things such as the civil rights movement culminating in legislation to address the cancer of racism in the country, the antiwar movement that grew up around the controversies of the Vietnam war, the emergence of the drug culture, the sexual revolution and especially the recognition of sexual discrimination and the ongoing work to bring about equality between the sexes, and the modern world's plague called HIV/AIDS. As a lover of athletics, I shall never forget the spring day in 1953 when Roger Bannister of England became the first person to run the mile distance in under four minutes, and thereby opened the gates for other middle-distance runners to push the record lower and lower. During my lifetime I saw Hank Aaron break the home run record of Babe Ruth. I watched the emergence of basketball players such as Kareem Abdul-Jabbar and, more recently, LeBron James; also Serena Williams in tennis. Those who came and went during my time include Jack Nicklaus in golf, Wayne Gretzky in hockey, Mike Tyson in boxing, Walter Payton in football, and the great Brazilian Pelé in soccer.

Something else has happened during a period that covers the second half of my life, and that has radically changed my world. I am not even sure what to call it—the information explosion, the digital age, or something else. I fear that I have not handled it well, and I am quick to admit that I am intimidated by this always-moving new frontier. Not long ago I awoke to the realization that I never feel as inadequate and old as when I am with my two sons. They are not responsible for my feelings. It is just my experience of being the only one in the room who is not interacting with a smartphone, along with all of the other new things that fit into that category. The words *fossil* and *relic* come to mind.

Clearly there are many aspects of this new age to be highly valued; our whole culture has been changed and many things I could not have imagined thirty years ago are now common fare. One day, for example, I was in the city of St. Petersburg, Russia, and I needed some cash. So I took my cash card, from a credit union in a small California town, found an anytime teller machine, followed the prompts, and received a handful of rubles—ready to face another day in Russia. Today such things are taken for granted.

The computer has, with a few exceptions such as North Korea, turned our world into what Marshall McLuhan called the global village. I saw a shepherd boy and his sheep in the Palestinian city of Nazareth. "Such a first-century pastoral scene," I mused. Then, as I got closer to my shepherd, I saw that he was wearing designer jeans. The new technology has made it possible for us to communicate with people of all circumstances in virtually any part of the world, and at a moment's notice.

The Maasai cattlemen of East Africa's Great Rift Valley must tend their cows in an area where prides of lions go out at night to find solutions to their hunger. So the herders drive their charges into primitive enclosures called kraals. These kraals are surrounded by walls made from thorn-burdened acacia branches and seem to keep the cows from becoming lion fodder. And during the night the cow herders keep track of hungry lion prides with the invaluable assistance of global positioning systems. Today's fishermen gain the upper hand on denizens of the deep with the use of radar and sonar. When I went fishing as a boy I carried my fishing pole and a can of worms, hoping to attract the attention of unwary fish that might or might not even be there.

In most instances these days I no longer need to give people driving directions; I simply give the address and assume that Garmin will take over from there. My son, pastor of a new church in the San Francisco Bay Area, used to refer to his smartphone as his office. And I knew that he was in touch with things better and more efficiently than was I with my cumbersome file cabinets. My other son draws working drawings of construction projects with the invaluable assistance of his Mac. These two examples illustrate the scope of the computer's helpfulness—from the architect to the pastor.

Most who read what I write about the digital age see these examples as commonplace characteristics of life. They say that the day is coming when the medical people will make us new body parts as we need them. How long we will live when that happens, I do not know. By the way, I am glad to know that human body parts are to be generated by computers because I am also told that the day is not far off when the computer will drive our cars. When this happens I suspect that we will need more parts.

There is also the work of the astrophysicists with their Hubble Space Telescope, along with computers whose voracious appetites consume vast amounts of information and tell us about the universe in which we are microscopic at best. For me this raises the question of infinity, and more specifically, how minute my world is in this boundless space that we call the universe. I have yet to meet the person who can explain infinity to me. For me, time and space *without end* are beyond comprehension. In the midst of this pervading insignificance the ancient scripture asks the probing question: "What is man that you are mindful of him, and the son of man that you care for him?" The answer? "You have made him a little lower than God, and you have crowned him with glory." The passage comes from a poet whose work is included in the Hebrew Bible's collection of psalms.

What this sentiment means to me is that, in spite of all the things that can add to my feelings of inadequacy, the Almighty yet thinks of me as having worth and importance. And I am still trying to live out the implications of this fact as I relate to others who share my world with all of its challenges and inscrutability.

Our older son, Michael, majored in English at his college in Virginia—a small Methodist institution called Emory and Henry. On one occasion he traveled to England with his college choir. In London he had opportunity to visit Westminster Abbey and hear Archbishop Desmond Tutu of South Africa. Michael sat with some of his friends in what the abbey calls Poets' Corner. It does not get much better than that for one who is reading English literature as a college major.

The lesson to be taken from the archbishop's sermon on that occasion is that I, as a member of the human race, am meant to *genuflect* to others. It sounds somewhat strange at first, but what the speaker was suggesting is a specific posture for living. To genuflect is to honor the other person, to bow in respect, to defer to the other by bending my knee. In my own tradition it means that when I look at another human being who shares my world, no matter his or her station in life, I see something of the image of God and it means, "Handle with care." If my world is to endure then this must be my posture. Such a simple lesson it is. And yet, it is also singularly profound in its ramifications, and it fits in every place and at all times. No matter what outside forces, historical events, or personal experiences shape me, it is appropriate, it fits. This I have learned over the years of my life.

10

AM I MY BROTHER'S KEEPER?

My actions surprised me. It was something I would not normally do, and it caught me cold. So, let me explain. In the past decade I had faced significant losses in my life with deaths of two members of my immediate family. First, it was my sixty-four-year-old brother and then, a year later, my mother at age eighty-five. So I was left with memories of these special loved ones along with photographs of them taken over many years.

In our home there is a bookshelf that is partially dedicated to displaying these pictures. It's a collection of family portraits spanning four generations of the Hoffman and Morgan clans, as they say, "the quick and the dead." This gallery is the first thing you see as you enter the house from the downstairs entrance. To some who view our rogues' gallery, the arrangement looks messy, even a bit helter-skelter. But my response is that this is how it is with all families—somewhat messy. Those families who appear to be completely tidy have simply found ways to conceal the truth. I freely admit, however, that there is often a temptation to romanticize things when talking about our families, to make ourselves look better than we really are, especially when we speak about the ones who are no longer with us.

Walking past the photos on the bookshelf that day I was thinking about my brother as I viewed a portrait of my mother. In that instant it was as if she were really there before me, and I spoke to her. I simply said, "I won't forget him." I was referring to my late brother. It was a statement of fact and it was more than that; it was also a promise. The way it came about is what took me by surprise; it is not my custom to talk to photographs. So, what follows is an attempt to keep a promise I made to my mother posthumously, but a promise I consider both valid and compelling, no matter how I came to it.

He was Willard and Erma's first child, born September 19, 1935. The place was a little town called Coronach in southern Saskatchewan near the US border. He and I were both born there, but it was many years before I learned that Coronach, the town, was named after a famous English racehorse in the mid-1920s. There is no way to find any significance in that bit of trivia, but I suppose there may have been a resident of the town who benefited from the horse's victories. I hope so, because in those days the people of that place needed good luck as much as or more than anyone in the country.

A few weeks before my brother's birth, Erma's father, Benjamin Carey, was killed in a car accident close to the international border crossing between Montana and Saskatchewan. Willard, the soon-to-be father and son-in-law to the now-deceased Ben Carey, was notified of the accident and instructed by the doctor not to let his twenty-year-old pregnant wife know of the tragedy. She was Ben Carey's only daughter and the doctor feared that such traumatic news might compromise the pregnancy and put the lives of both mother and child at risk.

Decades later Father told me that the situation in which he found himself was unbearable. He said he would never have agreed to the doctor's orders had he known how untenable it would be to carry them out. He was forced to withhold information about Ben Carey's death from the one who loved him most, to secret within himself the burden of this loss. He had to deal alone with the simultaneous feelings of elation in anticipation of a first child and of desolation over the loss of a family member. What made matters even more difficult was his uncertainty over the wisdom of what the doctor had told him to do.

By the time my mother knew of her father's death the funeral had already taken place. She had no opportunity to share those important early hours and early days of painful loss with her mother and younger brother, let alone to say any sort of good-bye to her father. The anger and hurt she suffered from that experience were with her all the days of her life. To her credit, I believe she never felt that the new baby boy was in any way a replacement for the father she had lost so tragically. She outlived both of them, her father and her son, and until the end her love for each was loyal and passionate. From each she derived great joy and treasured memories.

My brother was named after one of Father's cousins, a Pennsylvanian who was called Delbert. And he was given two other so-called middle names: Willard after my father and Benjamin after the grandfather he never knew. So there you have it—a name that only a mother could love: Delbert Willard Benjamin Hoffman. I think my brother disliked each of those first three names on its own, but the combination of all three was more than he could endure. He called himself Del, and he signed his name on all documents, official and otherwise, as Del W. B. Hoffman.

One of my early memories of Del has to do with the birth of our sister on September 17, 1943. She was named Erma Lorraine but was soon called Bunnie, a nickname given to her by our father and one she has carried into her seventies. I was not quite four years old when my sister was born. As I was too young to attend school, I was often bored with being alone, and anxious for my brother to return from Willoughby Elementary School. On the day of our sister's birth, I was sitting on the tractor anxiously awaiting my big brother's arrival as he made his way down the long driveway from the gravel road to our little farmhouse. When he was finally within shouting distance I delivered the annunciation: "Del, we have a new baby sister!" His response was an unenthusiastic, "I know." His words disappointed me and I always wondered how he knew; he had spent the day at his school away from telephones or any other form of communication. But about fifty years later Mother told me the truth. In fact, he did not know. But older brothers don't like getting important news from younger brothers. Most of us, especially older siblings, want to be the first to get the scoop on things. It's a common human trait.

I remember Del. And when I think of my brother as a youngster and throughout his adulthood as well, I think of a short, stocky, and strong person with a winsome personality. As a boy he had thick, coal-black hair that resisted any of his efforts to bring it under control. Some of the old photos show him with a pompadour, his hair slicked straight back against the dictates of nature as though waiting for the first opportunity either to stand at attention or fall out or spring forward. And when you understand that the hair was close cropped on both sides and at the back, showing lily-white skin, you get the impression of a bizarre black wig on a white marble Grecian bust. It was a fearsome sight, a tonsorial disaster, and I'm sure Del wished many times that he could dispose of any evidence of that first attempt to come to terms with the hairy conundrum that occupied the top of his head.

It doesn't really matter. As so often happens, my brother morphed into a handsome man. His hair settled down and became one of his assets, especially as it began to gray. Not only that but, after a health scare, he dropped excessive weight, quit smoking, ate a healthy diet, drank moderately, and paid attention to his underlying lust for life. Once you spent some time with him enjoying the infectious smile and the sparkling eyes you could only conclude that you had to clear space for him in your life. Here was a man worth knowing.

Although Del and I pursued much different paths in life and saw each other infrequently, we somehow maintained a close relationship—this in spite of the fact that one of the toys of our childhood was a set of boxing gloves given to us by our father. Now, years later, I can still feel the soft leather and recall the pleasant smell of those dark brown boxing gloves. And I remember how perfectly they fit when the laces were properly tied. My dad was keenly interested in boxing, the so-called sweet science. He would relate stories about John L. Sullivan and Gentleman Jim Corbett as well as Jack Dempsey and Gene Tunney, all former heavyweight champions of the world. With my dad I remember listening to radio's Don Dunphy, the preeminent voice of boxing matches in those days, as he described the contest between champion Joe Louis, the Brown Bomber, and challenger Joe Walcott, known in the fight game as Jersey Joe. It was December 1947, years before the advent of television in our home, as Dad and I pulled our chairs close to the radio and listened to the broadcast from Madison Square Garden in New York City. The fight went the distance, fifteen rounds, and when it was all over Joe Louis, who had been knocked down twice, was declared the winner. It was a controversial decision and I was among those who believed that Jersey Joe should have been awarded the victory. He had been robbed not only of the win but also the heavyweight champion of the world title that went with it. But I simply had to live with the injustice; no one listens to a seven-year-old boy in matters as important as professional fighting.

But let me tell you more about those boxing gloves. Del was four years older than I—smarter, bigger, stronger, and much less vulnerable. To his credit, he would do what is known in the sport as pulling his punches, holding back and not allowing the punch to be delivered with its full force. Had he not done this I probably would not be around to tell you what a magnanimous spirit he was as he pulled punch after punch. As things turned out, however, there were those times when one of his blows would get away from him and not rest until it had landed squarely on my jaw. To Del's credit, he never knocked me out, but after the errant left jab or right uppercut had found its mark I would cry, Del would apologize, Mother would place cold compresses on my head as I lay on the couch, and I would eventually ratchet up my courage to try it again. I don't know, but I cannot imagine that those accidental blows did anything to help me in my forty-five-year battle with migraine headaches. I do know that when I at long last boxed against someone my own size it was relatively easy. In fact, I met a retired gentleman a few years ago who told me that when we were kids we had boxed each other and that he ended up on the floor. I did not remember but I did feel a little embarrassed.

In those days we heated our house with firewood and cooked our food with a wood-burning stove. Fortunately, there was plenty of firewood available from the lumber mills of the Pacific Northwest. So every summer without fail the trucks would come and deliver about five loads of wood, dumping it wherever Father instructed. To my brother and me that woodpile looked like Mount Everest and we were charged with the task of stacking the wood neatly so that it would dry in the summer sun. We probably could have accomplished the assignment in one day, but we both hated stacking wood. It was the bane of our summer days. We would stand around the woodpile arguing, fighting, complaining, picking slivers out of our hands, and doing everything other than what we were out there for in the first place. I have no memories of ever finishing the assigned job. What I do remember is that Mother would ultimately give up on us and finish the work herself.

You have to remember that we lived in a unique time and place, so our experiences were far different from those who followed us. We lived in a world of wringer washing machines, clotheslines upon which we hung our newly washed clothing and waited for it to dry in the open air, and outhouses that might have to be visited any time of the day or night. In the cities we were accustomed to milkmen with their horse-drawn wagons delivering milk in one-quart glass bottles. With our hand-cranked butter churns we made our own butter out of cream from our own cow. We were familiar with the plaintive call of steam-powered freight trains whistling their presence as they coursed along the valley of the mighty Fraser River. On a few occasions we rode streetcars in our cities and trams in the outlying areas, while on family outings we rode in our Model A Ford car on unpaved roads and two-lane highways. Some of us lived in houses with linoleum-covered floors and with root cellars where we kept potatoes and other perishable supplies through long winters. Enclosed within our properties there might be a pigsty, a cattle barn, or a chicken house. We experienced the Saturday night bath in a washtub placed in the kitchen near the relative warmth of the cookstove, we attended one-room schoolhouses with a number of grades meeting simultaneously under the leadership of one teacher, and we endured the discipline of government war rations from 1939 until 1945. I count it a singular honor to inform you that my first airplane ride was in a biplane. I sat on my father's lap as from the clear blue sky we enjoyed a marvelous view of our world for fifteen minutes. The cost for the ride along with a lifetime memory was three dollars.

In order to supplement the family income we kept two hundred chickens and marketed the eggs. But this was also a no-win situation for Mother. In this instance the responsibility for cleaning the eggs before they were sent to market was handed over to my sister and me. As a middle child I got to help both the oldest and the youngest of my siblings. And once again the arrangement looked much better in theory than it did in practice. Both Sister and I hated cleaning eggs so we tended to fiddle away the time and in the end Mother did that job for us as well.

As I grew up I saw my brother as the strong one, able to do so much that I couldn't do, capable of working alongside my father as man with man, gifted in solving all sorts of problems, clever in his dealings with people of any age, and nobody's fool. I later described him as a man with a lot of street smarts. Yes, there were times when his style of living got him into trouble, but in the end he was seen as a credit to his community and as a successful and honest entrepreneur. As for the two of us, he and I, we were both glad to be brothers and we loved and respected each other. Of this I am sure.

For most of our adult lives Del and I lived far apart, he in British Columbia and I in California, some fifteen hundred miles away. From time to time during those years he would travel my way. When that happened he merely showed up, no advance notice, just a telephone call, usually on a Saturday, when he would inform me that he was nearby and was wondering if I had any plans for the next day. He might have known that his younger brother, a clergyman, usually had plans for *the next day*, which was Sunday. But how I would love to hear that voice on my phone again; how I would love to hear it any day of the week and any hour of the day.

One of the great gifts of my life is to know that my brother respected me and was proud of what I had done with my vocation. He even told me that he enjoyed hearing my sermons. And, though he had strayed far from the church of his childhood, I had the feeling that he and I were not far from being on the same page with the things that matter most in life. Here again, I wish our conversations over such things could have continued much longer than they did. I regret that the dialogue ended abruptly and I am also forever sad that in our senior years we could not fulfill plans to travel together, visiting some of the places we knew so well when we were children of our own shared yet distant past.

In many ways Del was a free spirit. But in most ways he took care of important matters. And, although he left high school before he graduated, he eventually went back to school and earned his diploma. Subsequently, he saw himself through the rigors of a university education at the

University of British Columbia. Along the way he worked a variety of jobs—gas and oil truck driver, service station attendant, heavy equipment operator, and oil pipeline grunt, to name a few. I believe his first choice would have been to be a Royal Canadian Mounted Police officer but, at a little over five feet six inches, he was deemed to be too short for the job. Still, he endeared himself to the local constabulary and sometimes rode with them as they made their late-night rounds policing the rural communities outside the city of Vancouver.

Following his university graduation he became a public schoolteacher and eventually a school principal. Prior to all of this he married his high school sweetheart, Mary Gorcak. Del and Mary's only child, a daughter, was born in 1972. They named her Carey-Jo after her two grandmothers. She was a precocious, privileged child growing up in the interior of British Columbia—a mystical land of mountains, valleys, lakes, and streams. Her life was filled with all sorts of activities, some planned by others and many birthed from her own creative imagination and abundant energy.

In early 1988 Mary tragically died of cancer. She was forty-nine years old, wife to Del, who helped nurse her with tender care through the final days of her life, and mother of a fifteen-year-old daughter who was bursting with energy and ready to take on the world. Soon after her mother's death, Carey-Jo competed for and won her weight class at a national judo competition and was declared the Canadian national champion. On a television interview out of Montreal and with great poise she dedicated her victory to her late mother, the most important person in her life.

By now my brother had left the field of education in exchange for a new life in the real estate business. Eventually, he opened his own office and did well, amassing various properties in and around the Windermere Valley in southeastern British Columbia. He married his second wife, Beverly Weir, a real estate agent, and he was seen as a fixture of the community. He had robust health, lots of friends, a good standing in his Rotary Club, time and money to travel, and, best of all, a growing admiration and love for his daughter as a young adult. And, although she would always in some way be his little girl, she was now much more than that. He had accepted the fact that she was a quick-witted, capable, self-assured, and independent woman who could make her own way in the world. She could manage; she could take her lumps like anyone else. She was launched and now he and this special daughter could begin to know each other in an infinite variety of ways. They could love each other without conditions and look forward to times spent in each other's company. They were not there yet, but that was the promising direction of this father and daughter path.

But it was not to be. It happened in the month of December, 1999. By this time my brother and his wife owned a second home in Arizona. They were members of an informal group of Canadians known as snowbirds—people who migrate south in the winter to escape the harsh weather. They had also developed a love for Mexico and its people, particularly for the state of Oaxaca in the southern part of the country. So, with the lofty intention of learning to speak the Spanish language and with their fifth wheel truck and trailer laden with gifts collected for Mexican children from Del's service club, they crossed the border into Mexico. Del called me a few days before he left the States and it was easy to hear the pride and joy in his voice; he was excited by the prospects of this trip. He especially looked forward to delivering bicycles and clothing to children in Oaxaca. I was happy for him. It wasn't the first time he had been able to touch something deep within his own soul, something that could only be found by reaching out to the needs of others.

But that telephone conversation was the last time we talked. Of course, neither of us knew it at the time. And in the days that followed his call I busied myself with the demands of leading my Southern California congregation through the season that leads up to Christmas that the church calls Advent. We had come to the third Sunday of Advent's four Sundays, a day focused on the subject of joy. I spoke about joy in our morning services and, later in the day, I shared a story with the children at an evening of festivities.

Somewhere in my files is a manuscript of the sermon I wrote for that Sunday. It was preached under the playful title, "Tickled Pink," and it was an attempt to help us think honestly and truthfully about the meaning of joy and its place in our lives. As always, my musings on the subject were offered to a room full of people whose lives ran the gamut from pleasure to pain, from contentment and peace to restlessness and emptiness. The reality is that whenever a person stands before others and speaks in a public forum there are as many audiences as there are people in the room. This is always the challenge I was aware of as I attempted to prepare for what they call the Sunday morning sermon.

The story I shared with the children in the evening of that same day was autobiographical. It told how, many years ago, the two Hoffman brothers—Del, age ten, and I, age six—set out to get a Christmas tree in the woods on our own family farm. It described how the Douglas fir tree was carefully chosen, how it was cut down, dragged through the snow, and finally set up in our old farmhouse with its ten-feet-high ceilings.

The story was a journey through part of my own nostalgic past in an age of innocent wonder. What I had no way of knowing as I related that memory of Del and me to the children of my church was that my brother—my big brother who carried the ax, who had the final word in choosing the tree, and who chopped it down for our Christmas elation—was no longer in the land of the living. His and his wife's lives had been violently taken from them not long after they headed south and left the United States behind. As I rhapsodized about yuletide bliss that third Sunday of Advent, their bodies lay among the sagebrush and sandy soil of the high desert in Sonora—two Canadians murdered by two Americans in the land of Mexico. But I was unaware of their deaths, so it was easy to generalize about the happiness of life, to be glib even when that was the last thing I wanted to be.

The news was conveyed to me by Sharon at noon on the Tuesday following third Advent. Sharon had answered a telephone call to our home from Canadian authorities in Ottawa and received the dreadful news first. Now there is no easy way to deliver such information to another person, but she did it with sensitivity and deep empathy, followed by unwavering support and love.

For me, it was impossible not to think about the scenario of the crimes that took the lives of my brother and sister-in-law. In such matters it is easy to get carried off into the land of conjecture, but in the days that followed I read reports of what had happened. They appeared in newspapers from Vancouver, newspapers that I had delivered to rural homes when I was a boy. And they appeared also in the Canadian national press, which told of how the suspects were apprehended, charged with the murders, tried, found guilty, and sentenced to sixty years' incarceration. All of this was carried out under the auspices of the Mexican judicial system, the sentence to be fulfilled in a Mexican prison.

Tragic news brings with it an impossible agenda of emotion and action all interwoven into an unworkable puzzle, a jumble of requirements and obligations reaching in every direction, and all undertaken with a colossal lump in the throat of life. So it was that I set about to respond. But I was not alone. Family and friends rushed in with help of all sorts. I was carried along by the people of my congregation. Friends from far away contacted me and spoke comfort over the telephone. Our cousins Larry and Martha made arrangements to be with Mother, to deliver the tragic news of what had happened to her son and daughter-in-law, and to take her to their home so she would not be alone. I'm sure they told her she could stay with them as long as she needed to stay. Meanwhile, an official in Tijuana, Mexico, made the trip east to the state of Sonora to identify the bodies. This meant that I, the one in closest proximity to the grisly scene of the crime, would not have to perform that distasteful task. We did what we had to do. Somehow we conveyed the unwelcome news to those who were most affected by Del's death—Carey-Jo; my mother, Erma; my sister Lorraine; and others.

A memorial was held for Del at my mother's church near Vancouver; another, a community gathering for him and his wife, was conducted in their hometown of Invermere, located in the Windermere Valley. I led the service for Del at Mother's church near the area where we had both grown up. And in this I was greatly assisted by my lifelong friend, David Carmichael. The people who attended formed a list of individuals whose paths had crossed our own over decades of time. It was a visit to our past and a tribute to my brother's memory. Our two sons, Mike and Andrew, and Lorraine's daughter, Lorri, and son, Tyree, all participated in the memorial. A special moment in the service was when Carey-Jo's aunt Joanna, Mary's sister, read a eulogy that she had written for Del. She did it with grace and sensitivity and with good humor. Another moment was when my brother's old friend Pat, at our request, stood and read the twenty-third Psalm—*the Lord is my Shepherd . . . even though I walk through the valley of the shadow of death I will fear no evil, for You are with me.*

I spoke at the memorial using notes from the sermon on joy that I referenced earlier. In such circumstances a preacher is pushed to the wall. Is there a reality to the joy of third Advent that holds its ground even though we stand by the grave of our loved one whose life has been meaninglessly ended? I believe there is and this is what I talked about. If it is true on Sunday it must also be true the other six days of the week. So there is such a thing as joy even in the moment of tragedy, but it is a muted joy, an incomplete happiness, an unfulfilled pleasure, a moderated taste of something yet to be.

Some people believe that in the moment of our death our whole life flashes before us. Who knows? Maybe it does and I wonder if it did for Del. In that fatal instant I want to believe that my brother's memory worked the miracle, recalling the essence of his earthly sojourn: the word of encouragement from his dad—the father's blessing that every son and daughter longs to hear; the embrace of his mother who could not and would not ever stop loving him; the strong and tender love of Mary, his first love; the birth of his daughter, *his* daughter; the humor and mischief of his beautiful sister; the enfolding arms of the brother he knew and did not know; the carefree days of his youth; the joys of home; the moments in the mountains with best friends; and the suspicion he and I had talked about—that God is much better than the way so many of his minions portray him. All this and much more I want to have been brought into clear focus for Del W. B. Hoffman, my brother.

Invariably there comes the time when the bereaved are expected to pick up the pieces and get on with their lives. So I returned to Southern California. I got home a day before the Christmas Eve service at my church. For years it had been my responsibility and privilege to speak on that occasion and I decided that this would be no exception. I could have turned things over to another person, specifically to my colleague Melanie Silva who, with her husband Bill, had given me unfailing support. But I made the decision that it would not only be good for the congregation to see that I was still involved in their lives at such a poignant moment, but that it would be good for me as well. In my case it was the right thing to do.

Three months after these events I decided that I needed to make a trip to Mexico to the place where my brother's life had been taken. I felt that it might help me put some of the pieces of this morbid nightmare in place, and I believe it did. But in order to do this I needed help, so I asked another colleague, Djalma Araujo, to go with me. I needed someone who spoke Spanish and Djalma, a close friend from Brazil and professional colleague, fit the bill perfectly. Subsequently two other cherished friends, Lothair Green and George Davis, heard what we were up to and announced that they were going, too. They did not ask permission; they simply declared their intent and I was moved by their support and by their sense that they needed to be there. So it was that the four of us, all Methodist clergy, set out on a Sunday afternoon in George's Volvo on our way to Tucson, Arizona, and on to Magdalena, Sonora, the next day. We carried with us two wooden crosses, two flowering potted plants, and a small stuffed rabbit sent to me from my sister Bunnie with instructions to have it left in the place where our brother died.

The police in Magdalena remembered the fatal event, knew where it occurred, and informed us that we should not go there alone. So two young officers were assigned to go with us and serve as our escorts. A few miles south of the town they pulled their pickup truck off the divided highway into a rest stop. This is where Del and Bev had stopped just three months earlier. This is where they were accosted by two young men, removed at gunpoint from their vehicle, directed to a secluded spot, and lost their lives.

Here my friends and I secured the small wooden crosses, placed the flowers, and situated the stuffed bunny at the cross for Del. With these arrangements complete we then stood together in sacred solidarity in the silence of this unsuspecting sanctuary, our two young escorts looking on. At the right time we turned our attention to our common prayer book and, as the book was passed from one to the other, we read what is called the Service of Death and Resurrection. At the right time I was finally overcome with emotion, I think the first time my three brothers had seen me break down. At the right time the clouds floating above us dropped their moisture, great tears of divine grief falling upon us in some sort of sacramental washing. Some of those raindrops fell on the prayer book that I now held in my hands; they left their mark so that in the years ahead, whenever I would officiate at a memorial or funeral service, I would run my fingers over those small indentations and remember. At the right time George shared an appropriate poem from the vast collection he has committed to memory, and I knelt at the foot of my brother's cross as into the sandy soil I scratched the word, *Amen.*

In some way such as this the church has gathered through its long history for support and affirmation whenever it faces its losses—the right thing at the right time.

Reflecting on my extended family at this moment, I am aware of a long list of those who have, as they say, preceded me in death. None of these deaths was as tragic and dramatic as that of my brother, but I believe that with each demise my own life is somewhat reduced. In most instances this is not necessarily a bad thing; it is normal, an inevitable chapter in nature's unfolding story. ". . . Any man's death," wrote John Donne, "diminishes me, because I am involved in mankind . . . " This is the sentiment of an English poet writing four centuries ago, and it is our common human experience, too. But it does not mean we are ultimately defeated, because, along with the diminishing there may also be a growing, an increase in the range and scope of our lives, as we recall the life of the one who has died and as we celebrate that life.

This does not mean that we should adopt an easy truce with this last enemy. I agree with the twentieth-century Welsh poet Dylan Thomas. In one of his most quoted passages he says:

> Do not go gentle into that good night
> Old age should burn and rave at close of day
> Rage, rage against the dying of the light.

Still, the very moment any one of us is born, we are dying, even if we do not embrace death as a welcome guest.

Some of us find comfort in our faith, but only when we push beyond the superficial and trite and ultimately disappointing answers that well-meaning consolation often seizes upon. Some find help from the philosophers and poets, and some from friends who, although they have no credentials in the field of bereavement, possess authenticity and honesty and wisdom in whatever they set out to do for us. These might be the ones Thomas Gray elegized in 1750 when he wrote: "Full many a flower is born to blush unseen."

Each of us is a unique traveler on the road called loss; we are each different from the other. I have told you a little about my journey, but more important than this I have tried to follow through on the promise I made to my mother having to do with her first son. I will not forget him.

11
RETURN TO AMERICA

When Sharon and I married in December of 1960, she had already completed her degree in piano performance and pedagogy. I still had a semester to finish before I would be awarded the bachelor of theology degree. So, while I put the finishing touches on my undergraduate requirements, Sharon taught piano on two very long days each week at a town called Eckville, located a few miles from Red Deer, Alberta. It was demanding work for her, made even more difficult by the intensity of the weather and the fact that she had to drive an old Volkswagen Beetle over fifteen miles of snow-packed roads and through winter storms. As things turned out, she continued teaching through much of our married life and until she set her talents to creating the "Roses of Sharon" greeting cards. These she marketed through a variety of outlets, including the gift departments of Nordstrom stores on the West Coast. Sharon always thought that I was overly busy with serving different churches, but I think she was just as busy with her work and with being a mother to our sons, not to mention a wife to me.

At the end of summer 1961, following my graduation from college, we made our way to Kansas City, Missouri, where I was to complete three years of seminary education and be able to put "bachelor of divinity" behind my name.

The person who gave me vital assistance at this juncture was an American man named Willard Taylor. He was president of my Canadian college when I entered in 1957 but left to teach at the seminary in Kansas City, Missouri, before I graduated. During Willard's brief tenure as college president he was granted a PhD in biblical studies from Northwestern University in Evanston, Illinois. So, when I enrolled at the seminary he was already there, and he took me under his wing. He advised me on how to get the most out of my studies, gave me generous doses of encouragement, and bolstered my confidence. He also chose me to be his reader during my final year as a seminarian. What this meant, among other things, is that I graded students' papers for some of his classes and, on one occasion, filled in for him as lecturer. I am humbled by and indebted to Willard Taylor for the trust and grace he gave me during my seminary days.

In the late summer of 1964, with seminary now behind me, I was asked to come back to the Canadian college as a teacher. The school's efforts to secure a new professor for the fall of 1964 had failed, so I was seen as one who could fill in temporarily. By this time the school had been moved nine hundred miles east of the old college town of

Red Deer to the city of Winnipeg, and I was hired with the understanding that I would be there for one year.

Winnipeg is the nearest thing you can get to Siberia without actually being in Siberia. Winter in Winnipeg is an annual test of character and endurance for its inhabitants. One frigid morning I stepped outside to head for my office when the temperature was sixty degrees below zero Fahrenheit. And this was before they had factored in the wind chill. I heard of one resident who wanted out. I'm sure there were many who shared the same sentiment, but this man had a plan. He announced that he was going to attach a snow shovel to the front of his car and drive south until someone asked him what it was, and that is where he would stay to live out his days on Earth.

Apparently, they could not secure an authentic professor at my old college so they settled on me. I was to fill in until someone suitable could be located and offered a permanent position on the faculty. So I was a stopgap measure. I was twenty-four years old and the students were calling me Professor Hoffman. It was ludicrous, a farce, even after I had convinced many of them simply to call me Chuck. It would have been more fitting for them to call me "Professor Stopgap," so that none of us, they or I, would lose focus on the reality of that arrangement.

Despite the shortcomings, the one-year deal turned into six years and during this time I think I set a record for number of different courses taught in the shortest amount of time. A sampling of what I was made responsible for includes the following: Introduction to Psychology, Survey of the Old Testament, Survey of Christian Doctrine, European

History, Psalms and Wisdom Literature, Introduction to Philosophy, The New Testament Letter to the Romans, and Systematic Theology. Whatever they asked me to do I did, or at least tried to do. I thought this was how it all worked. In fact, I once counted more than twenty different courses that I *taught*, and I use the word loosely, during those six years from 1964 to 1970. I suppose the students might have legitimately referred to me as "Professor Catchall."

In addition to this unrealistic teaching role at the college, I was also the teacher for an adult Sunday class at one of the local churches and I was athletic director and dean of men at the college. I was president of our district church youth organization, giving me jurisdiction over the three prairie provinces of Alberta, Saskatchewan, and Manitoba—one thousand miles from east to west. These may have been the only days of my life when I could have felt proud of my professional worth, but I was too busy to notice.

During part of that time I was even janitor at the church we attended, and during all of that time I struggled with migraine headaches. If you have never had a migraine headache you can skip this section. These headaches began when I started school in 1945; they ended in 1991, a period of more than forty-five years. I cannot tell you how many of my weekends they ruined, how many times I was excused from school to walk home with pain as my only companion, how many hours I spent sitting alone in a dark room silently surviving the throbbing hurt, how many holidays the migraines took over my life. Nor can I tell you how many times I sought an answer to the question as to the purpose of this unwelcome and menacing cohort. I can tell you that I came down with a headache one morning when I was guest preacher at a nearby church. I took two very strong pain pills to help me get through the service. Whom can you believe when the leader preaches a sermon out of a drug-induced euphoria?

I really do not know how much damage I did during my six years of teaching at my alma mater, but I trust and believe that God will treat me mercifully. Also, if God has a sense of humor, and I cannot imagine it could be otherwise, then my antics must have provided more than a few good laughs. One thing that has helped me is the good grace of my former students who seem to have survived the ordeal without any lasting scars. More importantly, many of them went on to pursue graduate degrees and to distinguish themselves in a variety of professions. I do take a little pride in this.

It was during this time that I got to know Arnold Airhart, an ordained elder in the church, a Canadian, president of the college when I taught there, and a remarkable man. On one occasion, during a visit to my aging parents in British Columbia, I made a telephone call to Arnold who, by then, was retired and living in a nearby town. I had not seen or talked to him for years but he received me as a long-lost brother. I am grateful that, in the course of my call, I had the opportunity to thank him for his work and to tell him that he was still one of the best preachers I had ever listened to. Some years later he returned the compliment when he called me to ask if he could quote from my Christmas letter the next morning in his adult Bible class at the church where he worshipped and taught. I suppose these are small gestures, my compliments to him and his to me. But without them life loses something important; they are a necessary ingredient in any vital friendship. My own world has lost something by the fact that both Arnold Airhart and Willard Taylor are no longer with us.

Now, regardless of my being in a land of make believe during most of those days of *Professor* Hoffman, some wonderful things did take place. And there was nothing more wonderful than the birth of our first child in May of 1965. We named him Michael Charles, and by the time we left Winnipeg in 1970, he was the unofficial college mascot. Mike's brother, Andrew Craig, came on the scene in 1971 while I was serving as pastor of a small but challenging church in the greater Vancouver area and taking classes at one of the local universities. I remember sitting with a discussion group at Simon Fraser University, silently exalting in Andrew's birth but not feeling free to share my good news with the class. Such is the impersonal nature of too much of university life.

This is the place for me to say it: I am unabashedly proud of my two sons. The loving way in which they relate to Sharon and me, along with their friendship, is one of the great joys of my life. Each has married well and each is intentional in the business of being a husband and father—Mike to three and Andrew to four. Additionally, they are dedicated to their chosen professions, serve the needs of others, and are committed to a calling, a vocation from beyond themselves.

In 1972, when Mike was seven and Andrew just one year old, and after two long years of soul searching, Sharon and I decided to make some changes that would have significant bearing on the future course of our lives and on that of our sons. We decided to leave Canada for the United States. We also made the difficult decision to leave our current denominational affiliation and align ourselves with the United Methodist Church in the United States. In this endeavor we were greatly assisted by my seminary classmate, Lothair Green. A little history about Lothair and me: following our seminary graduation he went to Ireland to pastor a church and I returned to Canada to teach. We stayed in touch with each other via snail mail, both of us becoming disenchanted with our lot in life, a disillusionment that demanded we seek other options.

Lothair was first to make a move. He came back to the United States to undertake graduate studies at the School of Theology at Claremont, California, and to become an elder in the United Methodist Church. I was slower off the mark, but I knew what Lothair had done in answer to his dissatisfaction, and in due course I asked him to help me find refuge as an associate minister with the Methodists. This took a little time, but eventually he came through with the perfect answer to my request. In so doing, he played an essential part in my transition to a new religious and national identity. He also introduced me to David H. McKeithen, a seasoned veteran of pastoral ministry.

David was a Mississippi preacher with a spirit as big as the Mississippi River. With Lothair orchestrating things, I met David for the first time over the telephone, he in Southern California and I in western Canada. David was looking for an associate to join his staff at First United

Methodist Church in Escondido, California. He had heard from Lothair that I might be interested in the position and now he was interviewing me over the telephone. It was June of 1972. As we conversed that Monday morning he asked me some good questions. He must have liked my responses because it was not long until he said, "When can you come down and meet with our committee?" I responded with another question, "When would you like me to come?" He didn't miss a beat but said, "Oh, today or tomorrow." I said, "Let's make it tomorrow." And that is what I did.

I made my airline arrangements, flew to San Diego on Tuesday, met with the committee that evening, was offered the position, accepted the offer the next morning, and headed home to lead a Wednesday meeting at my church. As I boarded the airplane, Frank Sinatra could be heard singing over the intercom, "I did it my way." Whether that song was providential I have no way of knowing. But, it certainly felt that way to me—Frank Sinatra as God's mouthpiece.

After much difficulty with US immigration authorities we made our move to the small city of Escondido, which before this I had never heard of. There I assumed my responsibilities as associate minister at First United Methodist Church. At the time, the best I could do was to obtain a temporary work permit, which had a shelf life of one year. Sharon had located this possibility by way of a well-placed call to the American immigration authorities at the Vancouver International Airport. This meant that I was entering the United States with the same authorization to work there as that afforded Canadian professional hockey players drafted by teams in the United States.

However, if we could not obtain a better alien status during that first year we could be forced to leave the United States and return to Canada. A number of people gave us support and helped with our dilemma. Ultimately, it was the late US senator Alan Cranston who intervened and paved the way for us. The senator had been encouraged by a letter from David McKeithen. Among other things, David informed Cranston that he and the fourteen hundred members of his church would much appreciate the senator's help.

As I worked with and got to know David, I learned that he had served his country as an army chaplain in the Second World War. Following this, he returned to his home state of Mississippi, and became a beloved pastor and civil rights leader during the 1960s. He will always be one of my heroes, and I am honored to say that he was also my friend. By taking a stand against the racism around him, he risked not only his career but also his life. In time, he was forced out of his church and later found a church home as an associate minister at Pasadena First United Methodist. There he started over and made his mark in a new setting. Not only that, he also opened a path for other like-minded and disenfranchised Mississippi ministers to find a place to serve in California. With good humor and genuine respect these preachers were referred to as the "Mississippi Mafia." If that is so, then David was the godfather.

At the time of our move to the United States, Escondido was a city of about twelve thousand residents located twenty-five miles north of downtown San Diego. I was responsible for two youth groups and the church's overall education program from infants to adults. While working in Escondido, I took directed study courses in Methodist history, doctrine, and polity, and met the other requirements for ordination in the United Methodist Church. Also, during my time in Escondido I commuted to the seminary and completed an MA degree in Christian education. The trip to the seminary in Claremont was just over two hundred miles round trip. So, even though I was able to take two classes by attending only one day of the week, it took a chunk of time. Often, I would drive to Claremont the night before my classes, sleep on the floor of a friend's apartment, attend classes all the next day, and drive home in the evening.

I served as an associate at Escondido for nine years, during which time more than a dozen young men from our youth group made decisions to enter ordained ministry as their vocation. Years later, while I was serving another church and as I was celebrating my sixtieth birthday, my church made plans to join in the festivities. It was Sunday, October 10, 1999. That morning I followed the chancel choir as it moved down the center aisle, a processional that was our common custom. I made my way up the steps and into the chancel of the church before turning toward the congregation. And as I did so I looked into the faces of six of the men who had been part of my Escondido youth group and who had followed me, first into ordained ministry and now, as I walked into my church for Sunday worship. These men, replete with their clerical robes, now occupied significant positions in the church. They were all leaders of congregations with the exception of one who held an important office with the national church in Nashville, Tennessee. They had made arrangements to be absent from their own responsibilities that Sunday morning and had traveled great distances to be with me. I was deeply moved by their gesture; it was a gift that I shall never forget.

But going back to 1972 and my arrival in Escondido, I must say that this represents my return to America. Of course, my colleagues and friends will always think of me as a Canadian. But my Hoffman ancestor came to America in 1739, my grandfather moved from the United States to his Canadian homestead in 1910, and I moved back to America in 1972. This means that I represent a family sojourn in Canada of only sixty-two years out of a total of 275 years since my ancestor, John Peter Hoffman, settled our future in what was to become the United States of America. Today, after living in America for more than half my life and after being naturalized as an American citizen, I am legally a citizen of both countries, Canada and the United States.

My tenure at First United Methodist Church of Escondido ended in October of 1981, at which time my bishop appointed me to another "First Church," the First United Methodist Church of San Diego. There I would serve once again as an associate but in a much larger setting—nearing four thousand members. In many ways these next ten years were the most important of my career. Working on a large staff, I learned from my colleagues and came away with an enriched understanding of my calling. Most of this important formation and reformation came to me from Mark Trotter. He was our leader, the senior minister of that church, whose vision of ordained ministry was nurtured in a family of clergymen—his grandfather, his father, and his two older brothers—all of whom were distinguished ministers. Later, Mark and Jean's daughter Martha would be added to the list of Trotter clergy.

After graduating from Occidental College in Los Angeles, and after marrying Jean, Mark enrolled in the seminary at Boston University. Following completion of his seminary degree he took further postgraduate studies at the seminary and at Harvard University, most notably under Paul Tillich, George Buttrick, and Paul Lehman. During this time, he worked at Trinity Church Boston under the eminent Theodore Parker Ferris, the fourteenth rector of Trinity. Trinity's roots reach back in time to the year 1733, so this is a church with long traditions. These and other experiences were analytically filtered through the lenses of Mark's calling and of his learning. And through all of this he never lost sight of the fact that one day he would serve a local church as preacher, pastor, and teacher. In his case the happy result was that in each of these roles he led with uncommon wisdom and performed with exceptional skill.

It was my good fortune to arrive at that church just as Mark entered the prime days of his ministry. And while I may not have always been aware of it, I was to learn valuable lessons. Each Sunday morning I listened to an exceptional preacher and learned what it takes to put together a sermon that is worthy of the name. I watched one who had a gift for discerning those church issues that were vital from those that were merely annoying. I saw the strength of humility and the unequaled quality of grace. I was challenged to be a better leader. It was a postseminary experience, one I covet for all who attempt to navigate the rewarding, yet often treacherous, waters of ordained ministry.

One of the achievements that stands out from my years at San Diego is the founding of the San Diego School of Christian Studies (SDSCS). This school was built around the idea that laypeople ought to be afforded opportunities to examine their faith as adults. It was to be a way to assist laypeople by providing them with honest ways to study their religion and to embrace it with integrity. So, I invited a group of interested persons to work with me on the project.

There were ten or twelve members of that first board of the SDSCS. Eight were attorneys and our first task was to draft a mission statement for the academy. It was a most interesting challenge and we met it head on. In less than a year the school was born. I was the dean and I had the fascinating assignment of hiring teachers from universities and schools in the region. Our first teacher was Pastor Jack Lindquist, a Lutheran clergyman who taught at the University of San Diego, a Roman Catholic school. Jack is a gifted teacher and his class put us on the map. Subsequently, I received calls from highly qualified people asking me if they could teach a course in our school. They would recite their qualifications, including present assignments at prestigious schools, along with an array of graduate degrees to their credit. In those instances I listened to their claims, and had the luxury of being able to ask the serious question: "But are you a good teacher?" I knew that good teachers could conduct their classes outdoors under a tree if that's all that was available. Motivated students will listen to good teachers. Now, more than twenty-five years later, the school carries on with its mission.

That is all wonderful, but there is another cleric that I must tell you about before moving to another topic. His name is George Davis. George was a key part of the ministerial team at San Diego First, so he and I were colleagues, and he remains to this day a cherished friend. In many ways George is like David Enarson, the preacher who embodied such a winsome spirit at a time when I was still trying to decide if there was life beyond my call to ministry. George is retired now, but he continues to be effervescent, attentive, and sensitive in his dealings with all who have the good fortune to know him. He is effusive in his praise of others—a quality that endeared him to me and to so many over the course of his career.

At various times in my ministry I ventured into the field of drama. On a couple of instances, for example, at church functions I tried to portray Mark Twain in a stand-up routine. George thought it was the greatest idea since the proverbial sliced bread. And, although he could not personally attend my first performance, he acted as though I should receive the Oscar for my efforts. I have often been made to realize that when something good happens to me, George is more excited than I am. How could you not love a spirit such as his? He might suitably have been named *joie de vivre*. During the days of his ministry and beyond, my friend George has helped all sorts of people to carry on when they thought they had come to the end. He helped me to be professional and personal at the same time and ultimately to be a better minister.

There are so many others who played a special role in my life. Without them, my life would have remained unfulfilled. Was it merely my good fortune to have so many angels along the way, or was something else at work, an orchestrated campaign to help me fulfill the calling that shook me to the core when I was so very young? I suppose some of our questions do go unanswered and this may be one of them, a query that merely hangs there in midair, perpetually seeking resolution. I can live with that.

12

THREE FEET ABOVE CRITICISM

On July 1, 1991, about the time my forty-five–year battle with migraine headaches was mercifully coming to an end, Sharon and I left San Diego and moved to Encinitas, a coastal community in the northern part of San Diego County. Bishop Jack Tuell appointed me there to serve as senior minister of the United Methodist Church in Encinitas.

Encinitas is a relatively new city, resulting from the merger of the communities of Cardiff, Leucadia, old Encinitas, and Olivenhain. The church itself, laboring under the unwieldy name of San Dieguito United Methodist Church, was brought into being by the combining of two Methodist congregations with long histories in the San Dieguito region. To some residents Encinitas is a surfing center, while to others it is the flower capital of the world. To another group it is a manageable commute south to the city of San Diego and north to Orange County, as well as a desirable place to live and raise families. To Sharon and me it is a wonderful setting in which to enjoy retirement, do photography, write stories, play golf, entertain our grandchildren and their parents, and spend time with our friends. We have lived here twenty-five years, longer than any other place either of us has lived. This is our home and we love it.

Serving as senior minister of a church was new territory for me. Here I would be expected to preach each Sunday, something that I had not done since leaving Canada nineteen years earlier. Following a scholarly preacher who had regularly challenged his listeners with his own knowledge and insight was also a daunting task. Not only that, I learned later that there were some clergy in our conference who would have welcomed the chance to serve San Dieguito UMC, and some who felt it unfair that an associate minister was given the coveted opportunity. Of course, I did not agree with them, and would have argued that the years of my ministry in the city of San Diego with Mark Trotter and the rest of his staff provided me with unique preparation for this new assignment.

Writing and delivering sermons is not the only assignment facing the clergyperson; it is, however, the most important. During those years when I did not preach on a regular schedule, but only occasionally, I did perform the usual duties of the office: baptisms, the Eucharist, confirmations, weddings, funerals, counseling, visiting in homes and hospitals, and teaching. At one of my churches I sometimes conducted three weddings in one day. I am sure there were mismatches that did not work out—betrayals of the marriage vows, incompatibilities that surfaced in the ongoing give and take of married life. These and other things too often undermined the original lofty plans and, sadly, the marriages ended in separation or divorce. I am also sure, and thankful, that I always matched the right woman with the right man and that none of the brides ever awoke to the realization that I had married her to someone other than her intended.

When preachers get together they will sometimes swap tales of the extraordinary nuptials they have been part of over the years of their career. Here is one of mine. I do not remember their names but I do remember that the bride and groom were tall people. As you may know, I am not one of the tall people. On the golf course I often hear one player encouraging another player who is facing the challenge of a long putt: "Don't be short," they will be heard to say. At that point, I am always tempted to say, "Don't worry. I've been short all my life." But we are not talking about golf here; we are talking about a particular wedding, the wedding of two tall persons by a short clergyman. She was five feet ten inches tall, which means that by the time she put on her high heels she looked down at me from a great height. The groom was six feet eleven inches, which means that he lived in a different zip code than I. Describing this ceremony I have often said that, when it was over, I had married her navel to his kneecap. I cannot imagine that this couple kept any of the photographs showing the three of us standing together.

Early in my fifteen years at San Dieguito, I discovered that my new church had a positive sense of self. It was not a false pride but, rather, an encouraging sense of being on the right side of things. I am not sure how to explain it, but it was apparent in the various committees of the church as well as on Sunday mornings when the congregation gathered for worship. It was a refreshingly healthy self-assurance, which I was able to nurture and enjoy during my tenure as pastor. No church leader can ask for more, and I am appreciative of the ministers with whom I worked in Encinitas: Sam Sallie, Melanie Silva, James Dollins, and Winfried Ritter, along with numerous retired clergy who made my church their church home. Together we worked with an unusually gifted cadre of laity who moved the church forward and into the twenty-first century.

I suppose that when the universal church was first designed it was with the realization that there may not be enough effective ministers to go around. So another way to ensure the church's future needed to be devised. Enter the layperson. I have never ceased to be amazed by this vital part of the church. I doff my cap to those professionals and nonprofessionals who, after putting in long, hard days at their own work, surrender evenings and weekends to God's work.

Now, following the completion of my formal ministry, I find that it is not easy to write about it. I am aware that history needs to be told from the perspective of time. Simply relating the accomplishments of those fifteen years at my last assignment is unproductive. I tried taking that approach and it did not work; it was boring for me and I'm sure the same would be true for my readers. I needed another approach, so I decided simply to relate some of the important things that happened during that part of my life.

It was not as though nothing of interest took place. It did. Most notably, I got to see the congregation embrace a six-million-dollar effort to enhance the church's tired facilities and present a better face to the community. It was high time we did it. And I will never forget what someone said as we planned for our new facilities: "If I was a young parent and saw the state of our children and youth buildings," he said, "I would look elsewhere for a church; I would know that this one does not value the religious education of the younger generation." It was both an indictment and a challenge.

On the plus side I can say that, inferior as they were, we used our church properties well. A case in point is what is known throughout the region as the San Diego North Coast Singers. Early in my tenure as leader, exposure to the arts was seriously curtailed in the public schools. You know how it goes in so much of public education. First, we come to the realization that we don't have the resources to do everything. Second, we realize that there is no alternative but to eliminate extracurricular programs. Finally, we terminate the music and arts instruction. Interestingly and tellingly, we would never take seriously any suggestion to cut back on football programs or any other of the popular sports programs. With football and in a convoluted lexicon of values we choose an expensive program that numbs the mental capacities of a few, over other less expensive activities that enhance the mental capacities of the many. Studies have been done that prove the point. But, as is often the case, when we do not like the scientific findings we attack the discipline for something more comfortable or we ignore it altogether. Whatever it was, the study of music and the arts was being curbed in our region. Something had to be done, and it was.

The leader of our children's programs at the time was Carol Swartz. She made arrangements for the children of our church and community to take part in formal choral groups. The person whom Carol selected for the job was Sally Husch Dean, an energetic and gifted musician who enhanced our hopes in ways we could not imagine. There were others who shared the initial vision, others who helped to shape what came to be known as the San Diego North Coast Singers. Today the SDNCS have sung throughout the nation as well as internationally, including at Saint Peter's Basilica in Rome, as hundreds of young people have had restored to them their musical birthright. If you believe, as I do, that the arts is one of the Creator's gifts, then you will also understand why we were moved to do something about this gaping hole in our children's education.

For me personally, the fifteen years at San Dieguito represent a time when I learned how to preach. Some would undoubtedly question this assertion and others would agree with it. At least, that's what the listeners told me over the course of my time. They told me wittingly and unwittingly, but they did let me know. When it comes to preaching, people do.

It used to be said that when the preacher ascends the pulpit for the Sunday sermon, he or she is standing three feet above criticism. But times change. Not long after my arrival in Encinitas, a woman came to my office to talk about my preaching. It was a less than cordial visit. "What did we do wrong to deserve you?" she asked. And there was more, but that is the gist of what she had to say to me that day. Obviously, she had not heard that a preacher is exalted above analysis or censure at such a moment. It doesn't matter; she would have rejected the idea anyway.

Once she had the floor, my critic pointed out that I relied too heavily on the Bible. I told her that I made no apologies for that and that I had no plans to change my view of the relationship between Scripture and sermon. There was more to our conversation, but I have conveniently forgotten most of what else she had to say about me and my feeble attempts to preach. She left my office unfulfilled. She left me with a bruised ego; I felt as though I was failing the part of ministry that was most important to me. Some of us are like that—one wheel squeaks and we assume they all do.

However, I did not quit. I went back to work with renewed vigor, and I am honest to admit that, as bad as it seems, one item on my agenda was to prove my antagonist wrong. I probably failed her on that one, too.

Preaching sermons based on the Scriptures takes different forms. In some cases it is manifestly apparent that the discourse is Bible based. If, for example, the one writing the homily believes that every word of the sacred text carries its own otherworldly credentials then he or she will take great care to point out word meanings, variations, uses, historical and cultural nuances, and so on. The precise meaning of each word in its context is vital. Obviously, there is value to this discipline, but it does not always preach well. One of the dangers is that the address ends up sounding like someone reading a page from a technical journal that, in this case, is called a commentary. Or, to change the metaphor, it can sound like someone reciting the music theory that lies behind a great composition. When a concert pianist plays a concerto she does not dazzle us beforehand with all the scales she had to master before she could master the challenges of the piece in question. The discipline of the scales is integrated into the playing of the work of art.

Overemphasis on technical aspects of a text in the *presentation* of the sermon can result in our missing the forest for the trees. But let me be clear. This attention to precise meaning is indeed called for. My contention is that word studies and what is called literary criticism, though demanded by honest preaching, do not justify having the prominent place in the actual *delivery* of the message. I take my cue from the Hebrew/Christian Bible itself. These sacred writings form our faith. As with all great literature, they deal with the total human experience from cradle to grave. And they teach us of an otherworldly involvement in our lives both individually and corporately. The themes are big—life and death, hope and despair, light and darkness, gain and loss, right and wrong, joy and sadness, love and hate, success and failure, humility and arrogance, sin and salvation—and whatever else fills up the days and years of our journey on this special planet. This is why I could not agree with the person who complained of my reliance on the Bible in writing a sermon. The stakes are too high; the church is more than another service club striving to live up to its charter.

So that is the first and most important thing I learned during the time I stepped into the pulpit each Sunday at San Dieguito. Truthfully, I learned this before I arrived, but in writing and delivering the message each Sunday my learning was uniquely confirmed.

Perhaps there was a time when parishioners placed their parson on a pedestal. I am not sure. But I am of the opinion that by the time the churchgoers started to enjoy the roast beef dinner the guard came down; likewise, the preacher. Of course, those comments about the preacher and the morning sermon would not have been called *criticism*, but probably something more like *evaluation*, as in, "He did a masterful job of staying with his theme." Or *clarification*, as in, "Whatever did he mean when he said . . . ?" Or *support*, as in, "Pastor must have been overly involved with parish matters last week."

All of this reminds me of a 1936 movie called *The Green Pastures*. It is an African American story of creation, heaven, Noah's ark, and other biblical events, and it is one of my favorite movies. In one scene a little girl visits the pastor to pose a question that has been bothering her. He gives an answer. She leaves contented, commenting on how wise her pastor is. "How wonderful," she says, "I didn't understand a thing he said."

Before, during, and after my time as preaching minister I held the opinion that the preacher had to connect in a significant way with the listeners. Merely filling in the allotted twenty minutes of sermon time is not enough. In my case, I was to take responsibility for the pulpit of a church that placed high value on that part of its life that occurred each Sunday morning. Please remember, prior to my ministry in Encinitas I had spent two decades as an associate minister who preached infrequently. That regular assignment had been given to someone else, the pastor in charge or senior minister. Consider, too, that I was fifty-one years old as I started this new and final chapter of my professional service. I was an "old dog," and you know what they say about old dogs and new tricks. So the learning curve was significant.

Years before this, when I was attempting valiantly to teach college students, I prepared my lectures with one thought constantly lurking in mind: "What questions are they apt to ask me?" The result of this is that my preparation included a lot of time scurrying about for answers. It also meant that I ended up trying to do too much. Similarly, there was a point in my sermon preparations when I endeavored to do too much. I felt that I should cover all the bases, but the load was simply too much for me and the listeners to carry.

I learned that the preacher should remain "three feet above criticism" for about twenty minutes—some say that eighteen minutes is the optimum time length for a speech, as in the vastly popular TED lectures on the Internet. So I would say, "Make the point, develop it, play with it, breathe life into it, and quit." In the world of the Sunday sermon less is more. Once again, I began to understand this while still working as an occasional preacher called the associate. Delivering sermons at San Dieguito confirmed it. By following this general rule, the time and the minds of the listeners are respected and the preacher, who always walks away knowing that more could be said, leaves the results in hands that are bigger than his or her own. Even the preacher must exercise faith. It's all part of the process. A phrase that comes to mind says, "Let the chips fall where they may."

Something else that relates to this is what I call the "Sesame Street Generation." I am aware that other children's programs have replaced the iconic "street" but I believe that the point is still apt. How do preschool teachers keep up? How do they overcome this phenomenon of constant stimulation? For me it would be terrifying to stand before young children who have been exposed to the wonderful world of stimulation—Oscar the Grouch, Big Bird, and the endless creations of artists and writers until the child's mind is totally captivated. "How," I have asked myself, "Does the teacher follow such an act?"

And how does the preacher follow that act when a significant percentage of the congregation was weaned on the same Sesame Street agenda? This is a real challenge, and I take it seriously. For me, this means that, as I write a sermon, there is a sixth sense at work—a little voice that reminds me to lighten up frequently, tell a humorous story, include an illustration, or throw in an anecdote. In other words, be cognizant of our real world with its smartphones; laptops; Wikipedia; instant updates on news, weather, and sports; GoPros; multitasking; and the brief attention spans of the listeners. The ones who can stay with me while I deliver a dense doctrinal dissertation are in the distinct minority.

Some would disagree with me when I say it, but there is indeed an element of entertainment in this strange thing called preaching. Some public speakers come by this naturally, while for others of us it is a thing to be learned. I would say that humor is the salt of life; without it life is flat. And so is the sermon.

I have heard it said that the sermon is passé, a thing of the past that once had a place in the worship of the church. I do not believe this. I do wish, however, that *bad* sermons were a thing of the past—mine and those of others. I believe preaching might go out of fashion when stand-up comics can no longer charm their audience and make them laugh in the nightclubs of the world. But, until that happens, let the priests and clerics of the world pay the price to come up not only with something to say, but also the means to deliver it. When a speaker has something to say and can say it with style people will listen. Build it and they will come. Don't build it and they still might come, but there will be a restlessness that robs the church of its real role in the world.

Any of us who preach have been reminded of our shortcomings. It happened for me in a variety of ways, and dramatically one Easter Sunday. The services were over and, as I walked through the empty sanctuary, I could almost hear the building sigh with relief at an ending to the burden it had carried over the past few hours. Wandering through the debris of scattered worship bulletins, askew hymnals, and a few lilies that remained behind, I came across a newspaper that someone had left on a pew. It was lying open with the crossword puzzle completed. Although I cannot be sure what it represented, I've never forgotten it. If I were a teacher, perhaps of creative writing, I would have my students write an essay on the question, "What did the left-behind, completed crossword puzzle mean?" Think about it. I did. I suspect a man completed that puzzle and left it there as a sign that he was present for the Easter service, but he was there under protest. Perhaps his spouse talked him into it. After all, she had bought new clothes for herself and for the children and she wanted him to join them in another occasional sortie into the religious realm of the world. I wonder, was there anything in the sermon that caught his attention? Maybe something that caused him to think about a matter other than the puzzle? Or did he hear only those things that supported his conviction that religion was for the wounded and weak of the world? Who knows? There were no clues.

In my attempts to be an effective preacher I discovered that my audience was made up largely of what I call poets and pedants. Yes, poets sometimes get carried away in flights of fancy, while pedants plant their feet firmly on the ground and will not be moved by anything but literal truths, substantial stuff of the sort that makes its way into the scientist's test tube. Historically, it is the poets who drew up the plans for elaborate cathedrals; it is the pedants who built them. Statues and icons and ornate trimmings are products of the poet's unfettered mind; the marble and granite come from the pedants who compute ways of getting the material out of the mountains and into the hands of the artisans and sculptors.

If this is true, then the obvious inference is that both groups are needed in the church. Perhaps it can be summed up like this: the difference is found in what each type strives for. The pedant posits premises while the poet paints pictures. The effective preacher does both, because both kinds make up the church.

In my own case, I come down naturally on the side of the poet. What this means is that I must strive to compensate, to make things as reasonable as possible, even when I know that I deal in things that may not give themselves over to the neat formula or the airtight case. Authentic religion is not a crossword puzzle demanding exactness. It is a life to be lived, which inevitably has pesky loose ends resisting every effort to tie them up neatly. True religion is not something that can be left on the pew after the benediction; it is something to be carried into real life with all of its comforts and difficulties.

There is another aspect of the sermon that is very important to me. I suppose this is the place for me to say that I have always been uncomfortable with clerics who come across as having all the answers. My hunch is that this air of certainty is a thing that they believe they must project. Some of my group are of the opinion that this is what not only the congregation but even God demands of them. I disagree. In fact, it became a constant challenge to me *not* to give the impression that I had it all wired. Reflecting on my life as a preacher, I became convinced that honesty required me to preach up to my own doubts. Don't get me wrong. I believe that a little of this goes a long way. But I firmly believe that the disciple known as "Doubting Thomas" is in the Bible for a reason. As Saint Paul once wrote, "Now we see through a glass darkly." Certitude and faith may not be helpful comrades. I was told that George Buttrick, the great American preacher of another generation, maintained that every sermon should have a hint of heresy in it. What this means is that we not only embrace our doubts but we also question our certainties.

The truth is that those who position themselves three feet above criticism know that they walk a tightrope between doubt and belief. If it is true that none of us has the whole picture, then we will always struggle with our faith. Yes, the truth *will* set you free, but it might well upset you first. It might even lead you to despair, but it will finally be vindicated. This is the meaning of the great symbols: the exodus of the Hebrews from a land of slavery to the land of promise, the seed that dies so that it may live, the river of life that is always flowing, being born a second time, and especially the great symbol of resurrection to new life.

Preparing a sermon is very easy. It calls the preacher to shed light from a higher wisdom on all that seems mundane. And that calling is also the challenge of the sermon.

13

ON THE WAY TO THE CHURCH

It was a Saturday morning in the fall of 1972. It was only a few weeks since my family and I had moved to California where I began my ministry in Escondido. I was out collecting old newspapers for recycling in a borrowed pickup truck. The proceeds from this enterprise would be used for our youth program, one of my many responsibilities as the new associate at the church. I had just left Canada where I was a college teacher prior to assuming leadership of a small church near Vancouver in British Columbia. So this change in my professional status was a challenge. I had not only exited my native Canada for the United States, but I had also exchanged one small Protestant denomination with which I was familiar for another, much larger, organization about which I knew little. As far as my career in the church, it felt as though I had taken a giant step backward.

But I soldiered on with my new job. It was not easy. The young people in that church were divided among three different high schools. They carried school allegiances into the church group, didn't associate with those from other schools, and were generally pretty mean-spirited with each other. Not only that, there were times when only two youth came to the Sunday evening meeting, one a regular and one a visitor. But nine years later, as I readied to move into another assignment, we had a thriving youth group, one that the whole church was proud of and that would provide the United Methodist Church with some capable clerics to collect its newspapers on Saturday mornings and do other, much more important things in service to the church and to the world.

I remember one Christmas Eve at that church. This time I had been asked to entertain the children with a story. Not having an appropriate tale at hand, I decided to write one of my own. But I did not use it until after I had given it a trial run with my two young sons. As the three of us walked the two miles to the church I told my story, the one I would use that Christmas evening. Fortunately, the telling went well both times, but I was in for a surprise when we met for worship the following Sunday. As I greeted worshippers at the door a woman approached me, thanked me for the story, and said, "It was good to hear it again. I haven't heard that story in a long time."

I was not sure how to respond without embarrassing the woman or myself. However, her comment proves the accuracy of the ancient sage who once said that there is nothing new under the sun.

On very few occasions I received applause as I came to the end of a speech or a sermon. This could be encouraging. Of course, it could also be a spontaneous expression of relief over the welcome ending to the ordeal of listening. Early in my career, not long after my seminary days, I was invited to speak at a youth convention in the city of Calgary. I was promoted as the keynote speaker at a Saturday evening banquet for the youth of our district. But the evening wore on. My turn to address the gathering followed a long list of events, including a speech from one of the elected members of the provincial legislature.

At last I was turned loose to deliver my carefully constructed message. By now it was about nine-thirty in the evening. We had been sitting at those tables for three hours, the audience was weary, and I was more than a little concerned about my ability to rise to the occasion after all that had preceded my moment of truth. But soon after I started I was aware that things were going well. What I was saying resonated with my audience. And then it happened. A voice within me said, "Stop. Stop now. Sit down and put an end to this marathon." So I did as the voice advised; I put aside my notes and quit. And to those who sat around the banquet tables I said, "Well, that's half my little speech. Come back another time and I'll give you the rest of it." Then I sat down to enthusiastic applause.

Now you could say that they were thanking me for having the good sense to terminate the endless list of speeches. Perhaps so, but for me it was one of the finest moments in my experience of public speaking. What I heard was affirmation, the sort of thing that says a pronounced *yes* to what is being said by another. I had visited that special place where public speakers hope to go but seldom do whenever they ply their trade.

For the first twenty years of my ministry in California I was called on frequently to conduct marriage ceremonies. Early in those years a couple came to my office for counseling prior to their wedding. I do not remember their names, only that they were not young lovers, already giving evidence of the eroding effect time inevitably brings to all of us.

At some point in our conversations I asked the couple a little about their history. Had either of them been married previously? They each said yes and we went on to talk about that and other issues for a while. I wanted to feel good about these two people being married and to gain some assurance that this was a good decision on their part.

The ceremony took place at a resort in a little village nestled in the hills north of San Diego. That sounded fine, but when I got there on the day of the wedding I learned that the actual rite would be held in the bar. So began a series of misgivings for me. Old Jim, who came driving up to the dubious establishment a little late, played the piano. The groom had known him in the army. Some saloon patrons were playing billiards while others were bellied up to the bar. This was hardly the place to solemnize the vows of marriage. And the marriage license revealed that this was his third marriage and her fifth.

When it was time for the ceremony to begin, I physically manhandled the bridal couple and their attendants into place. The billiard balls were silenced, the contingent standing at the bar turned to face the proceedings, and some of the onlookers even wept at the appropriate moment. After I had signed the legal documents and attained signatures from the witnesses I got into my car and drove away. It felt as though I was fleeing the scene of a crime.

A few months later I bumped into the groom at a service station. I asked him how he and his wife were doing. "Not very well," he said. "We're getting a divorce."

I change the name of the protagonist for this next incident. He was a scientist, a great lover of life and a totally eccentric character. I'll call him Jasper. He came to my office to pick my brain over a number of issues, one of which was his firm belief in reincarnation. The reason for his unyielding confidence in this idea of re-embodiment was that it had happened to him so many times. His current and previous lives spanned at least six generations. That's what this scientist told me.

The unique thing about these personal experiences is that each one of his former lives ended violently. He remembered them all. Once he was eaten by a saber-toothed tiger. Another life ended in his beheading by guillotine, and so on; he spared no details about the numerous sordid ways in which he had died. As he finished this litany of terror he told me that on one occasion he had been drawn and quartered. "You know what that is, don't you?"

"I think I do," I replied. "They tie a horse to each of your hands and each of your feet and then . . ."

"That's right," he said. "And there's not a thing you can do about it."

"Jasper," I said, "you could have said 'whoa.'"

Both of us laughed as we brought the counseling session to an end.

There was a time when I thought it was my job to "fix" that sort of thinking; to help the person make adjustments or to help him understand that reincarnation was not really part of the Christian view of life and death. I suppose this would have been my approach early in my ministry. But in this case, after a lifetime of failures to deliver on such projects, I decided that discretion is truly the better part of valor. Jasper's faith was different than mine, but he was happy, so it seemed this was one of those times when I should simply entrust him to the Source of his life and leave it at that.

Jasper passed away not long after that time we spent together. I sincerely hope that if he does come back for another cycle on the wheel of life he doesn't announce that in one of his previous lives he died at the hands of a minister during a counseling session.

All churches are schizophrenic. As the previous story illustrates, churches have their share of what we call "characters," and the first church I served proves the point. One of them was an elderly woman who lived alone. I am sure she is gone now, but I called on her one day for a visit. Older people are often lonely and a visit by anyone, even a minister, often proves to be a good tonic. We made small talk for most of the time I was there trying to be helpful, and I suppose I said something about her never being alone, that the Lord was always present with her. I am sure she could have told me of more than a few times in her life when that didn't seem to be the case. But she was kind and said simply, "Yes, the Lord is a good man." The Lord is a good man. At a time when most people stressed the deity of Christ, maybe she knew something about Jesus the man that her preacher needed to hear.

There was another member of that same church who caused me no end of grief. In his own way, he was faithful to his church. In fact, until he got to know me he thought my coming as pastor was a good thing. But trying to work with that man nearly drove me out of the ministry and, I think, he would have felt that was a good thing, too. This fellow was all rules and regulations. That's how he was brought up and it seemed that concepts such as grace and second chances and compromise were anathema to him. I should tell you that this was all taking place in the early years of the 1970s, when the upheavals of the previous decade were catching up with the church. Of all things, people were even bringing guitars into the sanctuary, writing new songs, and generally trying to adapt to the times. The facts were that this character was born in the wrong century and the shifting sands of change were beyond his abilities to cope. He was not alone; that was the plight of many church people in those days.

In this case it was not entirely my antagonist's fault. Those of us who were supposed to be leaders had not sufficiently grounded such people in the great traditions of the church so that they could weather the arbitrary winds that blew across their lives and threatened all that they held to be sacrosanct. They were not in a place to distinguish between that which is sacred and that which is a sacred cow.

On the flip side of this was another character in the same church named Sol. His given name was Solomon but he preferred the shortened version and went by Sol. He was in his late forties when I arrived as his pastor, and he was one of my greatest supporters ever. At one point he had been a pastor himself, so he understood what it meant to lead a church. And he could still preach, and preach well when called upon.

Sol's life had been difficult. His first wife died when she and he were young. He suffered from Bell's palsy, which meant that part of his face was paralyzed, which, unfortunately, led some to conclude that his mind was impaired. Nothing could be further from the truth.

One Christmas Eve, after he had remarried and had built a new house for his family, that house caught fire. The volunteer firefighters came with their equipment but most of them were showing the effects of their Christmas celebrations. They were in no condition mentally or physically to tackle the fire and the house went up in flames. I don't know how Sol spent Christmas and Boxing Day that year, but as soon as that time had passed he began the formidable task of rebuilding his home.

Through all of his troubles this wonderful man never lost his endearing spirit. In private, I learned that he was one of the best tellers of stories to whom I have ever listened. Usually, these tales were about himself and some of his own experiences from the past, and he always salted them with just the right amount of self-deprecation. He endeared himself not only to his family, but also to those of us who knew him at that little church. The young adults especially loved Sol and cherished times when they could be with him, perhaps to enjoy one of the meals he cooked and the camaraderie that went with it.

At some point he had made the decision to leave the formal ministry and work as a layperson in the church. But prior to this he had served a small church in northern Canada. Such churches expected much of their ministers. In his own inimitable style, Sol told of a construction accident that claimed the life of a young man whose body was moved to a building at the church where it would be kept until the funeral. Sol was in charge, not only of the service, but of preparing the body for the internment. This was a challenge in more ways than one. It was winter and the building in which the body was kept had no heat, leaving the temperature below freezing. The victim lost his life at work, and his face was dirty, unshaven, and frozen. So Sol and his helper tried to rectify the situation with water for washing and a razor for shaving; they succeeded only in making things worse. Then the young man's brother arrived and introduced a further dilemma into the situation. He insisted on seeing his brother Bob before his burial. He made his wishes clear to Sol, and in spite of Sol's strong urging to "remember Bob as he was," the brother prevailed. But after he had seen Bob, he told Sol, "You know, I wish I had remembered Bob as he was."

The two years I served as Sol's pastor at that little church were some of the hardest days of my life. I wondered why I was there and felt defeated by so much of my life at that stage. Looking back in time I wonder if my purpose was fulfilled in the life of this one man who stands out like no other as I look back on my career. As we left he told Sharon that he felt as though he had been spiritually asleep for most of his life and that during those two years he was awakened. I still wonder if he was overstating his case, but he actually said that I had awakened him. There is no place to record such things in the church records. Nevertheless, they mean something important, something that transcends the usual things that get reported to the denominational leaders. The bottom line to those years of personal turmoil is that my path crossed with a man uniquely good and uncommonly talented, one whose life, a total of only fifty-four years, was too short and whose influence was too restricted. God bless you, Sol.

Next I want to write about Rodney, one who comes from a different time and place. Rodney frequented our church not on Sundays for worship, but on weekdays for money. He was a slim, good-looking, clever young man and he was a panhandler.

We were pretty slow on the uptake and it took us too long to realize that Rodney had our staff of five ministers on a schedule. Among other things, this meant that I would only see him every few weeks, during which time he was milking the system by seeing one or another of my colleagues. Eventually, we caught on to his scheme. I am pretty sure that Rodney was doing the same thing with other churches and social service agencies. Life was good on the dole.

To make matters even worse, he started introducing his buddies to his newfound bonanza. This raised the ante for those of us who were trying to be responsible with the church's finances, and once again he came to me for his allowance. I was ready.

It happened in the reception area of the church. There were three of us: the receptionist, Rodney, and I. How I did it I am not sure, but I backed Rodney up against the exit door, looked up at his face and, using language that I don't usually employ, I told Rodney to get lost. I figured that if he wouldn't respond to plain, unvarnished English, perhaps he might respond to the sort of language he used during most of the hours in his day. He did. We never saw him again. Perhaps it was against his religion to do business with a church that would employ a minister who behaved and spoke the way I did that day.

Over the years of my ministry there were many people like this young man. In fact, most of them were like him. But there were others, people who needed our help to get back onto their feet. And although they were in the minority, I fear that too often we failed them.

One time, in a bizarre turn of events, my youth director lost a car that had been donated to the church. I cannot tell you how he did this but I hope he was more responsible in his next job. Another time my colleague George and I stole a car off the streets of San Diego. This one I can explain.

It was Easter Eve and we had gathered before the service in the reception area of the administrative building. Laypeople and ministers visited with each other as we all waited to begin the Easter Vigil, an ancient practice of the church that is largely neglected by us Protestants. What we did not know as we milled around before heading for the sanctuary is that there was a thief in our midst.

We were a large congregation and there were none of us who could possibly know everyone else. The hard truth is that strangers may actually have attended that church for years. So our thief was safely blending in with everyone else. But he wasn't very smart. During this time when we milled around and waited for the service to begin, our thief attached his name to a sign-up sheet for those who were willing to assist with a homeless project. Not only did he sign his name, he also gave his address, which was a hotel in downtown San Diego.

When the service was over and it was time to go home, I looked into my desk drawer for my key ring. It wasn't there. So I looked to the parking lot for my car. It was gone. What had happened is that before we moved to the sanctuary for the Easter Vigil, our unwanted guest had sequestered himself in the administration building. While we worshipped he robbed. Besides my car and keys to my house, he took credit cards and cash from the ministers' offices. He made a thorough job of things and pulled away, not only with a car, but also with a treasure trove of loot.

But as things turned out we had his name and address. Now as I might have known, the law authorities were overwhelmed with crimes worse than what I had suffered. So I got little response from them about my loss. It took a few days for me to realize this and to know that if anything was going to be done I would have to do it myself. I remember a telephone conversation I had with a policeman.

"I think we have the name of this felon, and not only that, we have his address as well." I do not know if the lawman wrote any of this information down but he did listen to me.

"You know," he said, "In order for us to do anything you have to have seen this man driving your car and you have to prove that he was doing it without your permission."

"I see. Then tell me, are you going to follow up on this, or should I?"

"Why don't you do it?"

"OK, I will."

So that's what I did. I went to my friend and colleague George, who was in the next office, and I asked him to take me to the downtown address where we found an old hotel. And, lo and behold, parked there on the street was my car, which I simply unlocked and drove away. Not surprisingly, the car was a mess. Credit cards and other stolen goods were strewn all over the floor, the windshield was smashed, the seats were soiled, and the tank was full of gas. The robber had packed his belongings and was ready to leave town. So, I drove away with everything, including his suitcase full of clothes, his photograph, and a picture of his girlfriend.

As I made my way home I realized I was driving a stolen car. It was probably the first time that two members of the clergy had done such a thing.

Amazingly, the young thief was back at the church the next Sunday morning looking for "his" car. One of the custodians saw him and sent him away. By then, I had changed the locks so his key would not have worked anyway. Nothing in my seminary training prepared me for that one.

Finally, I want to share another incident that happened at the little church I served just prior to our move to California.

Not long before our move to that church a woman had lost her husband and was still in the early stages of her grieving. It was important that I visited at her home. So a time was arranged for Sharon and our five-year-old son, Michael, and me to make that visit. Prior to this Sharon had been reading Bunyan's *The Pilgrim's Progress* to Mike, and he had obviously been paying attention. During the time we were there with this woman who had been newly widowed, I struggled to listen and to say things that I thought might be helpful. Mike was quietly playing with his toys, seemingly miles away from our conversation. And then, unbidden, he got up and walked over to Mrs. Olsen.

"Has your daddy gone?" he asked her.

"Yes," she replied, "My daddy is gone."

He placed his chubby hand on her arm. "You'll see him again in the Celestial City."

It was time for us to go home. "A little child shall lead them." And he did.

14

Indefinite as God

No one person has an ordinary life. Each life is different and each has its memorable moments. Each plays a part in the family and its heritage. Even the life labeled ordinary has extraordinary meaning under the scrutiny of the one who lived it. One of my concerns is for my children and grandchildren to claim their unique limb of the family tree. Hopefully, these reflections will be helpful toward that end.

So what do these nearly three centuries of my family history offer me and my kin? Where have all these years led us? What has my own unique experience of life taught me? Well, for one thing and in a small way, I feel the excitement of an eighteenth-century German named John Peter Hoffman, who gambled his future on a land across the Atlantic Ocean—a land he had never visited and only knew from the various reports and letters he heard and read. None of them, however, told him all he needed to know.

One of the hurdles this man faced concerned the relationship between the settlers and the Native Americans. The settler, John Peter, sought some sort of accord between the two groups. And, although he joined what was called the Provincial Forces, an organization to protect the Europeans' lives and lands, there is evidence to suggest that he gained the respect of the native people.

I have done modest research on America's history of human enslavement and it appears that my ancestors, along with most of the Pennsylvanians, were not party to this despicable practice. For this I am profoundly grateful.

John Peter's second son, Christian, fought for the patriots in the Revolutionary War. He is my three-times-great-grandfather and it is conceivable that his son, Phillip, stood by the railroad tracks in northeastern Pennsylvania one day in 1865, as the assassinated President Lincoln's body was transported from the nation's capital to its place of burial in Springfield, Illinois.

Closer to my own time, I see Peter Hoffman, Phillip's son, patiently watching over my grandfather, William Cyrus, teaching him carpentry and marveling at how quickly the young boy learned the trade. William is the one whose tough mindedness and desperate prayer brought him and the young Frances through the terrible blizzard on the remote plains of Saskatchewan in 1910. He is the homesteader who built his sod house on that prairie, my father's first home and the place where he was born.

I have never been well-to-do in the common understanding of what that means. But in other ways I have much more than enough. I am wealthy in my friends, both personally and professionally. In so many ways they have enriched my life and left me better than when they found me. I am exceptionally well off with regard to my family—those who preceded me, my contemporaries, and those who now follow. The plantings of those first pioneers have taken root and the future looks hopeful and good. In looking back I can say that I sense purpose in my occupation of the space that has been mine for so many years.

The musings of the Scottish Presbyterian preacher, David H. C. Read, especially resonate with me. Dr. Read was pastor of the Madison Avenue Presbyterian Church in New York City from 1956 until 1989. He was a great preacher. Early in the Second World War he was taken prisoner at Dunkirk and spent the rest of the war years in a prison camp. At the time he was chaplain to the 51st Highland Division of the British Army. Read was also a prolific writer, and eventually came to write his autobiography. At the close of the first volume of this undertaking he affirmed his long-held faith when he wrote that, even during the years of his imprisonment as a POW, *the Center held*. The life and teachings of Jesus Christ were that Center and touchstone for the life of David H. C. Read. I can say the same. Over the course of my own life, a life that has known untimely and even violent death, crippling pain, and many failings, somehow the Center holds.

I say this but I am aware that this is not the experience of many who, at one time in their lives, embraced this faith handed down through the centuries. There are many would-be followers who have faced insurmountable hurdles in forming a healthy relationship with the Hebrew/Christian worldview and its God. This phenomenon, a reality for many, leads me to a number of conclusions.

I have come to believe, for instance, that there are far too many people who have fallen into the category of what I refer to as *disenfranchised Christians*. It is as though they don't qualify according to the rules—some of those rules being tenets that are often questionable and arbitrary. But we need these people; we covet their energy and their talents. The church needs to open its doors to these who have been left on the outside looking in. At the risk of being misunderstood, I say that there are times when orthodoxy is overrated.

In its long history the Christian church is guilty of erecting illegitimate barriers that exclude serious seekers while, at the same time, accepting many who have never probed the dimensions of this faith. The Hebrew prophet, Micah, asks the key question: "With what shall I come before the Lord?" The question is rhetorical; it leads to the prophet's own answer: "He has showed you, O man, what is good; and what does the Lord require of you but to do justice, and to love kindness, and to walk humbly with your God?"

This is enough. All the rest is personal preference.

It has been said that there are many who try to face the complexities of an adult world with a Sunday school understanding of their faith. In most cases it does not work. Such persons tend to take the nearest exit ramp, leaving the church behind. Many have an uneasy conscience about this but can see no alternative. I have met many of those who have chosen this path as they could see no other. They are often ones who embrace the ethical teachings of Jesus but who will not call themselves Christian; I have also met self-proclaimed

Christians who ignore these same teachings as they follow willy-nilly after the predominant culture. An example is that of such a man who was fully supportive of a controversial decision to use deadly force on another country. I asked this man how he reconciled his position with the teachings of Jesus. "Jesus was naive," he responded. End of discussion.

Somehow the group of people who come carrying their questions and misgivings ought to be invited into the fold or club or whatever you choose to call it. I call it the church and the inclusion of these individuals is one of my concerns.

A personal experience illustrates my point. We had invited interested persons to a luncheon to learn more about who we are and to receive an invitation to church membership. We had information to share and we set aside time for attendees to ask questions. One man called me aside because he was not comfortable posing his question publicly.

"I'm not sure what to do," he said. "I want to be honest and I also want to join this church."

"Tell me more."

"Well, it's like this. It's about the creeds, that part of our worship where we all stand together and voice our beliefs. I have trouble saying parts of those creeds with honest conviction. I guess I'm not sure what to do with my doubts and my reservations."

Now it was my turn to respond. And what I said was that there is room for him in our church. Not only that, there is also a welcome. I told this honest man that it would be better for him to ask his questions and address his doubts *within* the church fellowship rather than outside it. But best of all, he joined; he became an official member.

This man is not alone; he has many kindred spirits. The truth is that this kind of questioning is not inherently a bad thing. It is part of our essential humanity. The flip side of having faith is having doubt, and I'm not even sure you can have faith without doubt.

But this message gets lost, buried under ecclesiastical falderal. The skeptic among us is also the one upon whom we look with suspicion. We make requirements of all sorts—things that a person must believe on crucial as well as trivial matters before being allowed to join and be part of our group.

Very early in the church's life we are introduced to the patron saint of all those who pay attention to their uncertainties. His name is Thomas and his followers are legion. In fact, all of us are Thomas at some point in our lives. We are all like the confused man who responded to Jesus by saying, "I believe. Help me in my unbelief." But this is the natural way of things and we do not need to panic when it happens to us. A reading of the lives of the saints reveals that even those with robust faith had to come to terms with their own reservations; faith had to flourish in the face of those realities.

When I was twenty-five years old I suppose I thought I had it all figured out. Now, more than fifty years later, I know, I mean *really know*, less. This is not the way I would have scripted things. On my own I would have programmed faith to push for definitive answers until it arrived at a place called certainty. Now I believe that there is no such place, which is why I once told my congregation that I did not understand as much today as I did when I was much younger. From their own experiences of a life of faith they knew what I was talking about.

I am attracted to and challenged by the writing of Herman Melville in the classic novel *Moby-Dick*. In a brief chapter titled "The Lee Shore" Melville talks about the land toward which the wind blows and toward which it drives the ship. Under ordinary or calm weather conditions this land promises safety for the vessel. But when the wind blows powerfully toward the shore all is changed. Now the shore threatens disaster. To yield to the leeward wind is to ensure a catastrophe for the ship and her crew. The only truly safe place is the tempestuous sea, even with all of the storm's unknowns and ambiguities, its inscrutability and mystery and raw power.

As Melville wrote with such genius: "But as in landlessness alone resides the highest truth, shoreless, indefinite as God—so better is it to perish in that howling infinite, than be ingloriously dashed upon the lee, even if that were safety."

"Indefinite as God"—these are for me the captivating words. They are also fearful, and they mean that God remains to some degree in the realm of mystery, always a little beyond our reach, refusing reduction to any of our human formulae. Always there is more.

We are free to choose between the safety of the shore and what Herman Melville calls "the howling infinite." Today, the tone of many religionists, whether leader or follower, bends toward safety and peace and soothing tranquility; calm waters and safe ports are cherished. But it is a great act of faith to surrender one's soul to the unpredictability of the waves and the arbitrary nature of an open sea.

It is my belief that God is to be found in the tempest; my conviction that God is to be known in the risky and sometimes ragged edges of life over which we have little control and only partial answers at best. But, if we have the courage, it is there that we shall catch a vision of the Ultimate. That vision may be fleeting and incomplete and untidy, but it will be honest. It may raise as many questions as it does answers, but in the end it will be worth the risk.

The facts are that writers, scientists, philosophers, theologians, and others have all embraced the mystery that lies at the heart of things. Theologian David Buttrick once lamented that "the shiver of mystery no longer fills our worship." My own experience is that many preachers talk too much. And that is before they have even begun the sermon. Everything must be explained; nothing is left to chance. Liturgy must be augmented and symbols, no matter how hoary with age, must have the preacher's commentary.

Meanwhile, we head out to sea, to a world of complexities, difficulties, imperfections, intricacies, puzzles, and things that are never ended. Life forces us to grapple with issues that are multifaceted, nuanced, and sometimes simply inexplicable. And as if this isn't enough, we have to come to terms with our sacred book, wherein are passages that come under the category of "things I wish were not in the Bible."

All of this is true and all of it is a good thing. After all, if God is God then he cannot fit into my life as a talisman, a good luck charm. Surely, God must be bigger than my imagination. Still, I have encountered those who seem to think they have God in their hip pocket.

I love the ancient story of Moses as he is confronted by God speaking to him from a burning bush. As with us, Moses must have had some preconceived ideas as to how God communicates with the Creation, and a voice from a bush that was clearly afire but not consumed was not one of them. The main request, as far as Moses could discern it, was that he should take a leading role in freeing the Hebrew people from their slavery in Egypt. Actually, it was not a request from God but rather a commandment. And toward that end the first task for Moses is to confront the Egyptian pharaoh and order him to let the people go free. It's a tall order so Moses asks for something that will give him authentication in this lofty calling. He asks for God's name.

"I need to know," he says, "so that when the king asks who it is I represent I'll have an answer."

In response, God hands Moses a business card.

"My name is on the card," says the Lord. "This ought to clear things up for both you and the king."

Moses reads the card. On one side it says, "I am that I am." On the other side it reads, "I will be who I will be." This will clear things up?

So this man who will one day be given the Ten Commandments inscribed on two stone tablets scratches his head, strokes his beard, and, with just a small amount of knowledge, sets out to complete his assignment. His is the prototype of the call. And in the years to follow Moses will come to the conclusion that someone bigger than he is out there in the desert, not in a confining box but in a universe teeming with life.

God is found in the desert and also in the mountains and, for that matter, in all the places between the two. Personally, my sacred place is the mountains. I used to have a three-ring binder on a shelf in my office entitled, "The Holy Land." Most of the material in that binder, however, was about the mountains. More specifically, it had to do with the Sierra Nevada range of mountains in California—Mount Whitney, the John Muir Trail, Yosemite National Park, to name a few locales. I have been to the top of the iconic Half Dome twenty-eight times. My last trip was done on my seventy-third birthday in October 2012. The roundtrip hike to the summit from the valley totals sixteen miles and the elevation gain is over four thousand feet. Once, when it was still allowed, I went to the top in the darkness and, with my friend Arnie, I slept the remainder of the night there. I have been alone at the top, if only for a short time. I have pushed others to the summit, literally, and I have also brought them down when they were overwhelmed with fear. In nearly all of this I have felt a vicarious joy in seeing others exult in their accomplishment.

Now I'm sure that others have done that trek when they were older than I and many have done it more times. But I think there may be few for whom the mountain has played such a significant role.

With Sharon's help, I came at last to understand that my mountain had become a metaphor for my calling. Inviting people to join me on that hike was something like inviting people on the journey of faith. For all of us the key elements of life were there: the anticipation and anxiety; the fear of the unknown along with the enjoyment of the trail; the moments of pain, fear, and exhaustion; the exhilaration of success; and more. In other words, that hike mimics life.

During the last few years before I retired I took people from my church on this hike. And on the very last such outing my colleague, James, and I served Holy Communion there on the top of Half Dome. There were about fifty of us, and there was a wonderful surprise. A young woman from another hiking group saw what was happening that Sunday morning and came to us with a question: "Is this *closed* communion, or is it open to anyone who comes?"

James and I encouraged her to take part in this ancient sacrament of the church, to respond to the Lord's invitation, and to take the bread and wine of the Lord's Table. Happily, she joined us.

By the time we were ready to begin our descent back to the valley, we had served three groups. At the first serving we depleted all of our Methodist grape juice and bread. Fortunately, a Methodist man who taught Sunday school in the Roman Catholic church called me aside and told me that he not only had a chalice in his pack, but that he also had a small bottle of wine. Another man volunteered the bagels he had carried to the top for himself and his family. We used both wine and bagels.

Once again, our altar was a granite rock nine thousand feet above sea level and this time the elements were improvised—a most memorable Eucharist. Then, just as we were about to leave this church in the heavens, came two of my friends, Ray and Angel. Angel was exhausted from the long climb so she acutely felt the need to replenish her energy.

As an Episcopalian, this was for her one of the meanings of the Lord's Supper, its sustaining power in her life. It was a great joy to serve those two, our third table in the span of an hour, and one of my last acts as pastor of the church.

Finally, I share a Half Dome story that goes back to June of 1989. My college roommate, Don, and I had made plans to go together to the top. Don lived in Toronto so he and his wife, Beth, had traveled a long way to be with Sharon and me in California. Then, on the morning of the hike we awakened to a torrential rainstorm. We had planned this trip a year in advance. Don and Beth had flown from Toronto to San Francisco, and now the hike was off. But, by the time we finished our breakfast, the rain stopped and the sun came out. The hike was on.

Beth came with Don and me for the early part of the hike and then turned back to spend the day with Sharon. And as my friend and I continued over those first few miles we talked about the new job that he would assume at the end of the summer. He would take on formidable responsibilities as an international officer with the human aid group known as World Vision. So he was understandably feeling a little anxious about his future. Then, as we were deep in conversation, we somehow lost the trail and had to do some searching to get back on track. It was embarrassing for me but there was nothing I could do but deal with our temporary disorientation.

Not long after that and back on our course, we saw that the clouds were once again gathering, and it was not long until we found ourselves taking refuge from the weather. We were halfway to our goal, but it was much too dangerous in these conditions for us to proceed to the summit of Half Dome in the storm. In fact, records show that lightning has struck that granite mountaintop in all twelve months of the year. So we stopped in a protective thicket hoping for another change in the elements.

But it didn't happen, and after an hour of waiting we began to get cold. So I decided that we would resume our hike toward the top of the mountain until that point where I knew that the trail becomes totally exposed as it empties onto the bare stone. That way we would not only generate some heat to keep us warm, we would be poised to make the top if the weather turned favorable. You can imagine our disappointment when we finally reached the extremity of where we could safely go and the storm had not abated. We made it to the tree line but the rain kept falling.

And then, suddenly, it cleared. Rain stopped. Clouds lifted. The sun came out. Don and I made our way to the base of the granite dome where nine hundred feet of cable awaited to help us reach our goal. I thought we were home free, but we were not. Don panicked. Who can blame him? The cables were wet and cold. The granite was slippery. He doubted my sanity. He had gone far enough. He quit.

So I went on alone, leaving him to await my return. At first, I seemed to be the only person on top of the mountain, but soon two other persons joined me. They told me they had talked with Don as he awaited my return at the foot of the cables. They encouraged him to give it a try but they were not sure they had been successful.

I stayed at the top only a short time and, concerned that my friend would be getting cold waiting for me, I started my descent. Then, about halfway down, I saw him. He was on his way up, and I was thrilled as we met on that steep slope, climbed together to the top, and celebrated with something to eat and drink.

That is my story of what happened that memorable day in June 1989. Or is it? Allow me to tell the story again. Let me relate to you what really happened. It goes like this: Looking down at the two hikers, God thought of the day ahead and smiled. Over the past thirty years there had been few days such as this one. At some point in that span of time the boys had become men. And, although in each man the boy still lived, it was only rarely that he was allowed to surface.

This day was one of those times. And God, who had created boys, was ready for the challenge. For, as they filled their packs on the eve of their adventure, God was busy marking the trail with surprises. At dawn's first light there came a thundering through the skies, a drenching and washing of the valley with rain. It was a ploy, a little trick to let the hikers know who was in charge. And so, properly humbled but full of excitement, they set out.

The first leg of the journey was a feast of rock formations, cascading waterfalls and misty trails. All of it was now bathed in sunshine. And it was shared with Beth, a special third person whose presence was an early grace of the day. Undoubtedly, the brilliance of that early going was for her. But her departure signaled the arrival of menacing clouds.

God was now free to work his mischief. So, with one stroke of magic he pulled the trail from under their feet leaving them to track and backtrack and feel foolish. It was all part of the plan, a small wrinkle in the pattern of the day.

At the halfway point they paused to rest and savor their progress. Meanwhile, God moved through the little valley ahead, and as he moved he pulled the clouds into place. Gray clouds they were, dark gray, restless, and intimidating, while the two friends searched for shelter in the forest. Then, as the friends waited in a protective grove, they nourished their stubborn hopes, even as rain and fire filled the air, as lightning split through the turbulence, and as heavy clouds crashed their thunder against a darkening sky.

At the right time, at a moment before the chill could overcome their spirits, they heard a voice, and the voice told them to move out. Against the voice of nature and against the voice of reason it told them not to turn back, not yet. So, while other trekkers picked their way downward toward the main valley, the valley they had left earlier that morning, they continued their climb. And the rain continued to fall.

Then it happened. Breaking into the clearing at the tree line, they found that God was already there. And God was pulling back the curtain of clouds, dancing sunshine on the virgin snow, and casting warm and breezy light on the world. God had come out of hiding so that earth and sky, endless rocks and lonely trees, blue jays and squirrels and marmots offered their good tidings and pulled the climbers toward their prize. And the sun continued to shine.

Eventually, God would have the two men stand together on the summit that now was somehow theirs. But before that could happen there was one last surprise and, for one of them, one last lesson to be learned. It came unexpectedly in the form of cold cables and slippery stone falling far away into space. It was a metaphor, a symbol of the year ahead, which, as with the last of the climb, was to be faced with proper respect and care. So, while his friend went on, Don waited. He waited for as long as it took for God to clear the way and to send two angels of encouragement. In the waiting was the silence and in the silence was the stillness and in the stillness came the courage and from the courage came the climb.

At last the two friends met there in the middle of this mountain stairway, one friend welcoming the other to his favorite place, his holy land. And so, with the help of the cables, they worked their way together to the top of Half Dome. And the rock at last could be transformed. Now, the wine they shared became a Eucharist, a thanksgiving, a holy communion, and the stone on which they stood became an altar. And there they drank from the deep cellars of friendship; there they savored the splendid vintage of life as the sun shone upon them.

And God looked on the morning and the evening of this special day, and God said, "It is good. It is very good."

Now you ask me, "Isn't this a little far-fetched? Is it not presumptuous to say that God would clear thousands of square miles of storm clouds merely to provide two middle-aged hikers a nice day?"

Well, of course it is. It is ludicrous. God would never act that way. Never.

But who knows? Maybe she would.

Now we see in a mirror, dimly,
but then we shall see face to face.

Now I know only in part; then I will know fully,
even as I have been fully known.

Paul, the Apostle

47494232R00140

Made in the USA
Middletown, DE
26 August 2017